THE CAVE OF THE ANCIENTS

This book is the fruit of a long life, training culled from the greater Lamaseries of Tibet and from powers which were gained by a very close adherence to the Laws. This is knowledge taught by the Ancients of old, and written in the Pyramids of Egypt, in the High Temples of the Andes, and in the greatest repository of Occult Knowledge in the world, the Highlands of Tibet....

T. LOBSANG RAMPA

"The marvels he presents are reported with a great deal of good-humored gusto as though he is not forcing his views on us, but stating his tolerant goodwill."

Boston Sunday Herald

"What fascinates the reader is not only a strange land—and what could be stranger than Tibet?—but his skill in interpreting the philosophy of the East."

Miami Herald

Also by T. Lobsang Rampa
Published by Ballantine Books:

THE THIRD EYE

THE CAVE OF
THE ANCIENTS

T. Lobsang Rampa

BALLANTINE BOOKS • NEW YORK

Copyright © 1963 by T. Lobsang Rampa

All rights reserved under International and Pan-American Copyright Conventions. Published in the United States of America by Ballantine Books, a division of Random House, Inc., New York.

ISBN 0-345-27614-0

Printed in Canada

First Edition: March 1965
Thirteenth Printing: July 1993

To

**MAX AND VALERIA SOROCK
TWO SEEKERS AFTER TRUTH**

FOREWORD

This is a book about the Occult, and about the powers of Man. It is a simple book in that there are no "foreign words," no Sanskrit, nothing of dead languages. The average person wants to KNOW things, does not want to guess at words which the average Author does not understand either! If an Author knows his job he can write in English without having to disguise lack of knowledge by use of a foreign language.

Too many people get caught up in mumbo-jumbo. The laws of Life are simple indeed; there is no need at all to dress them up with mystic cults or pseudo religions. Nor is there need for anyone to claim "divine revelations." ANYONE can have the same "revelations" if they work for it.

No one religion holds the Keys of Heaven, nor will one be forever damned because he enters a church with his hat on instead of his shoes off. In Tibet lamasery entrances bear the inscription "A thousand monks, a thousand religions." Believe what you will, if it embraces "do as you would be done by" you will GET by when the final Call comes.

Some say that Inner Knowledge can only be obtained by joining this cult or that cult, and paying a substantial subscription too. The Laws of Life say, "Seek, and you shall find."

This book is the fruit of a long life, training culled from the greater Lamaseries of Tibet and from powers which were gained by a very close adherence to the Laws. This is knowledge taught by the Ancients of old, and is written in the Pyramids of Egypt, in the High Temples of the Andes, and in the greatest repository of Occult knowledge in the world, the Highlands of Tibet.

T. LOBSANG RAMPA

CHAPTER ONE

The evening was warm, deliciously, unusually warm for the time of the year. Gently rising on the windless air, the sweet scent of incense gave tranquility to our mood. Far away the sun was setting in a blaze of glory behind the high peaks of the Himalayas, tinting the snow-clad mountain tops a blood red as if in warning of the blood which would drench Tibet in the days to come.

Lengthening shadows crept slowly towards the City of Lhasa from the twin peaks of the Potala and our own Chakpori. Below us, to the right, a belated caravan of traders from India wended their way to the Pargo Kaling, or Western Gate. The last of the devout pilgrims hurried with unseemly haste on their circuit of the Lingkor Road, as if afraid of being overtaken by the velvet darkness of the fast approaching night.

The Kyi Chu, or Happy River, ran merrily along on its endless journey to the sea, throwing up bright flashes of light as tribute to the dying day. The City of Lhasa was agleam with the golden glow of butter lamps. From the nearby Potala a trumpet sounded at the end of the day, its notes rolling and echoing across the Valley, rebounding from rock surfaces, and returning to us with altered timbre.

I gazed at the familiar scene, gazed across at the Potala, hundreds of windows atwinkle as monks of all degree went about their business at the close of the day. At the top of the immense building, by the Golden Tombs, a solitary figure, lonely and remote, stood watching. As the last rays of the sun sank below the mountain ranges, a trumpet sounded again, and the sound of deep chanting rose from the Temple below. Swiftly the last vestiges of light faded;

swiftly the stars in the sky became a blaze of jewels set in a purple background. A meteor flashed across the sky and flared into a burst of final flaming glory before falling to the Earth as a pinch of smoking dust.

"A beautiful night, Lobsang!" said a well-loved voice. "A beautiful night, indeed," I replied as I swiftly rose to my feet in order that I might bow to the Lama Mingyar Dondup. He sat by the side of a wall and motioned for me to sit also. Pointing upwards, he said, "Do you realise that people, you, and I, may look like that?" I gazed at him dumbly, how could I look like stars in the night sky. The Lama was a big man, handsome, and with a noble head. Even so, he did not look like a collection of stars! He laughed at my bemused expression. "Literal as usual, Lobsang, literal as usual," he smiled. "I meant to imply that things are not always what they seem. If you wrote 'Om! ma-ni pad-me Hum' so large that it filled the whole Valley of Lhasa people would not be able to read it, it would be too large for them to grasp." He stopped and looked at me to make sure that I was following his explanation and then continued, "In the same way the stars are 'so large' that we cannot determine what they really form."

I looked at him as if he had taken leave of his senses. The stars *forming* something? The stars were—well—*stars*! Then I thought of writing so large that it filled the Valley, and so became unreadable because of its size. The gentle voice went on, "Think of yourself shrinking, shrinking, becoming as small as a grain of sand. How would I look to you then? Suppose you became even smaller, so small that the grain of sand was as large as a world to you. Then what would you see of me?" He stopped and looked piercingly at me. "Well?" he asked, "what *would* you see?" I sat there and gaped, brain paralysed at the thought, mouth open like a newly landed fish.

"You would see, Lobsang," the Lama said, "a group of widely dispersed worlds floating in darkness. Because of your small size you would see the molecules of my body as separate worlds with immense space in between. You

10

would see worlds rotating around worlds, you would see 'suns' which were the molecules of certain psychic centres, you would see a *universe!*" My brain creaked, I would almost swear that the 'machinery' above my eyebrows gave a convulsive shudder with all the effort I was expending in order to follow all this strange, exciting knowledge.

My Guide, the Lama Mingyar Dondup reached forward and gently raised my chin. "Lobsang!" he chuckled, "your eyes are becoming crossed with the effort to follow me." He sat back, laughing, and gave me a few moments in which to recover somewhat. Then he said, "Look at the material of your robe. Feel it!" I did so, feeling remarkably foolish as I gazed at the tattered old garment I wore. The Lama remarked, "It is cloth, somewhat smooth to the touch. You cannot see through it. But imagine seeing it through a glass which magnified it by ten. Think of the thick strands of yak wool, each strand ten times thicker than you see it here. You would be able to see light between the strands. But magnify it by a million and you would be able to ride a horse through it, except that each strand would be too huge to climb over!"

It made sense to me, now that it was pointed out. I sat and thought, nodding, as the Lama said, "Like a decrepit old woman!" "Sir!" I said at last, "then all life is a lot of space sprinkled with worlds." "Not *quite* so simple as that," he replied, "but sit more comfortably and I will tell you a little of the Knowledge we discovered in the Cave of the Ancients." "Cave of the Ancients!" I exclaimed, full of avid curiosity, "you were going to tell me about that and the Expedition!" "Yes! Yes!" he soothed, "so I will, but first let us deal with Man and Life as the Ancients in the days of Atlantis believed them to be."

I was secretly far more interested in the Cave of the Ancients which an expedition of high lamas had discovered, and which contained fabulous stores of knowledge and artifacts from an age when the Earth was very young. Knowing my Guide as well as I did, I knew that it would be useless to expect to be told the story until he was ready, and that was not yet. Above us the stars shone in all their glory, hardly dimmed by the rare, pure air of Tibet. In the Temples and Lamaseries the lights were fading one by one. From afar, carried on the night air, came the plaintive wail of a dog, and the answering barks of those in the Village of Shö below us. The night was calm, placid even, and no clouds drifted across the face of the newly risen moon. Prayer flags hung limp and lifeless at their masts. From somewhere came the faint clacking of a Prayer Wheel as some devout monk, encased in superstition and not aware of Reality, twirled the Wheel in the vain hope of gaining the favour of the Gods.

The Lama, my Guide, smiled at the sound and said, "To each according to his belief, to each according to his need. The trappings of ceremonial religion are a solace to many, we should not condemn those who have not yet travelled far enough upon the Path, nor are able to stand without crutches. I am going to tell you, Lobsang, of the nature of Man." I felt very close to *this* Man, the only one who had ever shown me consideration and love. I listened carefully in order to justify his faith in me. At least, that is how I started, but I soon found the subject to be fascinating, and then I listened with unconcealed eagerness.

"The whole world is made of vibrations, all Life, all that is inanimate, consists of vibrations. Even the mighty Himalayas," said the Lama, "are just a mass of suspended particles in which no particle can touch the other. The world, the Universe, consists of minute particles of matter around which other particles of matter whirl. Just as our Sun has worlds circling around it, always keeping their distance, never touching, so is everything that exists composed of whirling worlds." He stopped and gazed at me, perhaps wondering if all this was beyond my understanding, but I could follow it with ease.

He continued, "The ghosts that we clairvoyants see in the Temple are people, living people, who have left this world and entered into a state where their molecules are so widely dispersed that the 'ghost' can walk through the

12

densest wall without touching a single molecule of that wall." "Honourable Master," I said, "why do we feel a tingle when a 'ghost' brushes past us?" "Every molecule, every little 'sun and planet' system is surrounded by an electric charge, not the sort of electricity which Man generates with machines, but a more refined type. The electricity which we see shimmering across the sky some nights. Just as the Earth has the Northern Lights, or Aurora Borealis flickering at the Poles, so has the meanest particle of matter its 'Northern Lights.' A 'ghost' coming too close to us imparts a mild shock to our aura, and so we get this tingle."

About us the night was still, not a breath of wind disturbed the quiet; there was a silence that one knows only in such countries as Tibet. "The aura, then, that we see, is *that* an electric charge?" I asked. "Yes!" replied my Guide, the Lama Mingyar Dondup. "In countries outside of Tibet, where wires carrying electric current at high voltages are strung across the land, a 'corona effect' is observed and recognised by electrical engineers. In this 'corona effect' the wires appear to be surrounded by a corona or aura of bluish light. It is observed mostly on dark, misty nights, but is of course there all the time for those who can see." He looked at me reflectively. "When you go to Chungking to study medicine you will use an instrument which charts the electrical waves of the brain. All Life, all that exists, is electricity and vibration."

"Now I am puzzled!" I replied, "for how can Life be vibration and electricity? I can understand one, but not both." "But my dear Lobsang!" laughed the Lama, "there can be no electricity without vibration, without movement! It is *movement* which generates electricity, therefore the two are intimately related." He saw my puzzled frown and with his telepathic powers read my thoughts. "No!" he said, "just *any* vibration will *not* do! Let me put it to you in this way; imagine a truly vast musical keyboard stretching from here to infinity. The vibration which we regard as solid will be represented by one note on that keyboard.

13

The next might represent sound and the next again will represent sight. Other notes will indicate feelings, senses, purposes, for which we have no understanding while upon this Earth. A dog can hear higher notes than can a human, and a human can hear lower notes than can a dog. Words could be said to the dog in high tones which he could hear, and the human would know nothing of it. So can people of the so-called Spirit World communicate with those yet upon this Earth, when the Earthling has the special gift of clairaudience."

The Lama paused and laughed lightly, "I'm keeping you from your bed, Lobsang, but you shall have the morning off in order to recover." He motioned upwards toward the stars glittering so brightly in the clear clear air. "Since visiting the Cave of the Ancients and trying the wonderful instruments there, instruments preserved intact since the days of Atlantis, I have often amused myself with a whimsy. I like to think of two small sentient creatures, smaller even than the smallest virus. It does not matter what shape they are, just agree that they are intelligent and have super-super instruments. Imagine them standing upon an open space of their own infinitesimal world (just as we are now!) 'My! It is a beautiful night!' exclaimed Ay, staring intently upwards at the sky. 'Yes,' replied Beh, 'it makes one wonder at the purpose of Life, what are we, where are we going?' Ay pondered, gazing at the stars sweeping across the heavens in endless array. 'Worlds without limit, millions, billions of them. I wonder how many are inhabited?' 'Nonsense! Sacrilege! Ridiculous!' stuttered Beh, 'you *know* there is no life except upon this our world, for do not the Priests tell us that we are made in the Image of God? And how can there be other life unless it is exactly like ours—no, it is impossible, you are losing your wits!' Ay muttered bad-temperedly to himself as he strode off, 'They could be wrong, you know, they could be wrong!'" The Lama Mingyar Dondup smiled across at me and said, "I even have a sequel to it! Here it is:

14

"In some distant laboratory, with a science undreamed of by us, where microscopes of fantastic power were available, two scientists were working. One sat hunched up at a bench, eyes glued to the super-super microscope through which he gazed. Suddenly he started, pushing back his stool with a noisy scrape upon the polished floor. 'Look, Chan!' he called to his Assistant, 'Come and look at this!' Chan rose to his feet, walked across to his excited Superior and sat down before the microscope. 'I have a millionth of a grain of lead sulphide on the slide,' said the Superior, 'Glance at it!" Chan adjusted the controls and whistled with startled surprise. 'My!' he exclaimed, 'it is just like looking at the Universe through a telescope. Blazing sun, orbiting planets . . . !' The Superior spoke wistfully, 'I wonder if we shall have enough magnification to see down to an individual world - I wonder if there is *life* there!' 'Nonsense!' said Chan brusquely, 'of course there is no sentient life. There *cannot* be, for do not the Priests say that we are made in the Image of God, how *can* there be intelligent Life there?' "

Over us the stars wheeled on their course, endless, eternal. Smiling, the Lama Mingyar Dondup reached in his robe and brought forth a box of matches, treasure brought all the way from far-off India. Slowly he extracted one match and held it up. "I will show you Creation, Lobsang!" he said gaily. Deliberately he drew the match head across the igniting surface of the box, and as it flared into life, he held up the blazing sliver. Then blew it out! "Creation, and dissolution," he said. "The flaring match head emitted thousands of particles each exploding away from its fellows. Each was a separate world, the whole was a Universe. And the Universe died when the flame was extinguished. Can you say that there was no life on those worlds?" I looked dubiously at him, not knowing what to say. "If they were worlds, Lobsang, and had life upon them, to that Life the worlds would have lasted for millions of years. Are *we* just a stricken match? Are *we* living here, with our joys and sorrows—mostly sorrows!—

15

thinking that this is a world without end? Think about it, and we will talk some more tomorrow." He rose to his feet and was gone from my sight.

I stumbled across the roof and groped blindly for the top of the ladder leading down. Our ladders were different from those used in the Western world, consisting of notched poles. I found the first notch, the second, and the third, then my foot slipped where someone had spilled butter from a lamp. Down I crashed, landing at the foot in a tangled heap, seeing more "stars" than there were in the sky above and raising many protests from sleeping monks. A hand appeared through the darkness and gave me a cuff that made bells ring in my head. Quickly I leaped to my feet and sped away into the safety of the enshrouding darkness. As quietly as possible I found a place in which to sleep, wrapped my robe around me and loosed my hold on consciousness. Not even the "shush-shush" of hurrying feet disturbed me, nor did the conches or silver bells interrupt my dreams.

The morning was far advanced when I was awakened by someone enthusiastically kicking me. Blearily I peered up into the face of a hulking chela, "Wake up! Wake up! By the Sacred Dagger, you're a lazy dog!" He kicked me again—hard. I reached out, grabbed his foot and twisted. With a bone-shaking jar he fell to the floor yelling, "The Lord Abbot! The Lord Abbot! He wants to see you, you cross grained idiot!" Giving him a kick to make up for the many he had given me, I straightened my robe and hurried off. "No food—no breakfast!" I mumbled to myself, "why does everyone want me just when it is time to eat?" Racing along the endless corridors, swinging round corners, I almost gave heart-failure to a few old monks doddering around, but I reached the Lord Abbot's room in record time. Rushing in I dropped to my knees and made my bows of respect.

The Lord Abbot was perusing my Record and at one time I heard a hastily suppressed chuckle. "Ah!" he said, "the wild young man who falls over cliffs, greases the

16

bottom of stilts, and causes more commotion than anyone else here." He paused and looked sternly at me; "But you have studied well, extraordinarily well," he said. "Your metaphysical abilities are of such a high order, and you are so far advanced in your academic work that I am going to have you specially and individually taught by the Great Lama, Mingyar Dondup. You are given an unprecedented opportunity by the express command of His Holiness. Now report to the Lama your Guide." Dismissing me with a wave of his hand, the Lord Abbot turned again to his papers. Relieved that none of my numerous "sins" had been found out, I hurried off. My Guide, the Lama Mingyar Dondup, was sitting waiting for me. Eyeing me keenly as I entered, he said, "Have you broken your fast?" "No, Sir," I said, "the Reverend Lord Abbot sent for me while I was yet asleep—I am hungry!" He laughed at me and said, "Ah! I thought you had a woebegone look as if you were being ill used. Be off with you, get your breakfast and then return here." I needed no urging—I was hungry and did not like it. Little did I know then although it had been predicted!—that hunger was to follow me through many years of my life.

Refreshed by a good breakfast, but chastened in spirit at the thought of more hard work, I returned to the Lama Mingyar Dondup. He rose to his feet as I entered. "Come!" he said, "we are going to spend a week at the Potala." Leading the way, he strode out of the Hall and out to where a groom-monk was waiting with two horses. Gloomily I surveyed the horse allotted to me. Even more gloomily he stared at me, thinking less of me than I of him. With a feeling of impending doom I mounted the horse and hung on. Horses were terrible creatures, unsafe, tempermental, and without brakes. Horse riding was the least of any accomplishment that I might have possessed.

We jogged down the mountainous path from Chakpori. Crossing the Mani Lakhang road, with the Pargo Kaling on our right, we soon entered the Village of Shö - where my Guide made a brief stop, then we toiled up the steep steps of the Potala. Riding a horse up steps is an un-pleasant experience, and my main concern was not to fall off! Monks, lamas and visitors, an unceasing throng of them were trudging up and down the Steps, some stopping to admire the view, others who had been received by the Dalai Lama Himself thought only of that interview. At the top of the Steps we stopped, and I slid gratefully but un-gracefully from my horse. He, poor fellow, gave a whinny of disgust and turned his back on me!

On we walked, climbing ladder after ladder until we reached the high level of the Potala where the Lama Ming-yar Dondup had permanent rooms allotted to him near the Room of Sciences. Strange devices from countries the world over were in that Room, but the strangest devices of all were those from the remotest past. So, at last we reached our destination, and I settled for a time in what was now my room.

From my window, high up in the Potala, only one floor lower than the Dalai Lama, I could look out upon Lhasa, upon the Valley. Far off I could see the great Cathedral (Jo Kang) with golden roof agleam. The Ring Road, or Lingkor, stretched away in the distance, making a com-plete circuit of Lhasa City. Devout pilgrims thronged it, all coming to offer prostrations at the world's greatest seat of Occult learning. I marvelled at my good fortune in having such a wonderful Guide as the Lama Mingyar Dondup; without him I should be an ordinary chela, living in a dark dormitory instead of being almost on top of the world. Suddenly, so suddenly that I emitted a squeak of surprise, strong arms grasped mine and lifted me in the air. A deep voice said, "So! All you think of your Guide is that he gets you high in the Potala and feeds you those sickly sweet confections from India?" He laughed down my protestations, and I was too blind, or too confused to realise that he knew what I thought of him!

At last he said, "We are in rapport, we knew each other well in a past life. You have all the knowledge of that past life and merely need to be reminded. Now we have to work. Come to my room." I straightened my robe and put back my bowl which had fallen out when I was lifted into the air, then I hurried to the room of my Guide. He motioned for me to sit, and when I was settled, he said, "And have you pondered on the matter of Life, on our discussion of last night?" I hung my head in some dismay as I replied, "Sir, I had to sleep, then the Lord Abbot wanted to see me, then you wanted to see me, then I had to have food and then you wanted to see me again. I have had no time to think of *anything* today!" There was a smile on his face as he said, "We are going to discuss later the effects of food but first let us resume about Life." He stopped and reached out for a book which was written in some outlandish foreign language. Now I know it was the English language.

Turning over pages he at last found that which he was seeking. Passing the book to me, opened at a picture, he asked, "Do you know what that is?" I looked at the picture, and it was so very ordinary that I looked at the strange words beneath. It meant nothing at all to me. Passing the book back I said reproachfully, "You know I cannot read it, Honourable Lama!" "But you recognise the picture?" he persisted. "Well, yes, it is just a Nature Spirit, no different from anything here." I was becoming more and more puzzled. What *was* it all about? The Lama opened the book again and said, "In a far-off country across the seas the general ability to see Nature Spirits has been lost. If one sees such a Spirit it is a matter for jest, the Seer is literally accused of 'seeing things.' Western people do not believe in things unless they can be torn to pieces or held in the hands, or put in a cage. A Nature Spirit is termed a Fairy in the West—and Fairy Tales are *not* believed." This amazed me immensely. I could see Spirits at all times and took them as absolutely natural. I shook my head to clear some of the fog out of it.

The Lama Mingyar Dondup spoke, "All Life, as I told you last night, consists of rapidly vibrating Matter generating an electrical charge, the electricity is the Life of

Matter. As in music there are various octaves. Imagine that the ordinary Man in the Street vibrates on a certain octave, then a Nature Spirit and a Ghost will vibrate at a higher octave. Because the Average Man lives and thinks and believes on one octave only, people of other octaves are invisible to him!" I fiddled with my robe, thinking it over; it did not make sense to me. I could see ghosts and nature spirits, therefore *anyone* should be able to see them also. The Lama, reading my thoughts, replied, "*You* see the aura of humans. Most other humans do not. *You* see nature spirits and ghosts. Most other humans do not. All very young children see such things, because the very young are more receptive. Then as the child grows older, the cares of living coarsen the perceptions. In the West, children who tell their parents that there has been a game with Spirit Playmates are punished for telling lies, or are laughed at for their 'vivid imagination.' The child resents such treatment and after a time convinces himself that it was all imagination! You, because of your special upbringing see ghosts and nature spirits, and you always will—just as you will always see the human aura."

"Then even the nature spirits who tend flowers are the same as us?" I asked. "Yes," he replied, "the same as us except that they vibrate faster and their particles of matter are more diffused. That is why you can put your hand right through them just as you can put your hand right through a sunbeam." "Have you ever *touched*—you know, *held*—a ghost?" I queried. "Yes I have!" he replied. "It can be done if one raises one's own rate of vibrations. I will tell you about it."

My Guide touched his silver bell, a gift from a High Abbot of one of Tibet's better known Lamaseries. The monk-servant, knowing us well, brought—not tsampa, but tea from Indian plants, and those sweet cakes which were carried across the high mountains specially for His Holiness, the Dalai Lama, and which I, just a poor chela, enjoyed so much. "Reward for special efforts at study" as His Holiness had often said. The Lama Mingyar Dondup

20

had toured the world, both in the physical and the astral forms. One of his very few weaknesses was an addiction to Indian tea. A weakness which I heartily endorsed! We settled down comfortably, and as soon as I had finished my cakes, my Guide and Friend spoke.

"Many years ago, when I was a young man, I scurried round a corner here at the Potala—just as you do, Lobsang! I was late for Service, and to my horror I saw a portly Abbot blocking my way. He was hurrying too! There was no time to avoid him; I was rehearsing my apology when I crashed right through him. He was as alarmed as I. However, I was so bemused that I kept on running and so was not late, not *too* late, after all." I laughed, thinking of the dignified Lama Mingyar Dondup *scurrying!* He smiled at me and continued.

"Late that night I thought about it. I thought 'why shouldn't I touch a ghost?' The more I thought about it the more determined I was that I *would* touch one. I laid my plans carefully, and read all the old Scripts about such matters. I also consulted a very very learned man who lived in a cave high in the mountains. He told me much, he put me on the right path, and I am going to tell you the same, because it leads directly to the theme of touching a ghost."

He poured himself some more tea and sipped awhile before continuing. "Life, as I told you, consists of a mass of particles, little worlds circling around little suns. The motion generates a substance which, for want of a better term, we will call 'electricity.' If we eat sensibly we can increase our rate of vibration. A sensible diet, none of the crank cult ideas, increases one's health, increases one's basic rate of vibration. So we come nearer to the ghost's rate of vibration." He stopped and lit a fresh stick of incense. Satisfied that the end was glowing satisfactorily, he turned his attention again to me.

"The sole purpose of incense is to increase the rate of vibration of the area in which it is burned, and the rate of those within that area. By using the correct incense, for all are designed for a certain vibration, we can attain certain results. For a week I held myself to a rigid diet, one which increased my vibration or 'frequency.' For that week also I continually burned the appropriate incense in my room. At the end of that time I was almost 'out' of myself; I felt that I floated rather than walked, I felt the difficulty of keeping my astral form within my physical." He looked at me and smiled as he said, "You would not have appreciated such a restricted diet!" "No," I thought, "I would rather touch a square meal than any good ghost!"

"At the end of the week," said the Lama my Guide, "I went down to the Inner Sanctuary and burned more incense while I implored a ghost to come and touch me. Suddenly I felt the warmth of a friendly hand on my shoulder. Turning to see who was disturbing my meditation, I almost jumped straight out of my robe when I saw that I was being touched by the spirit of one who had 'died' more than a year ago." The Lama Mingyar Dondup stopped abruptly, then laughed out loud as he thought of that long-past experience.

"Lobsang!" he exclaimed at last, "the old 'dead' lama laughed at me and asked me why I had gone to all that trouble, when all I had to do was to go into the astral form! I confess that I felt mortified beyond measure to think that such an obvious solution had escaped me. Now, as you well know, we *do* go into the astral to talk to ghosts and nature people." "Of course, you spoke by telepathy," I remarked, "and I do not know of any explanation for telepathy. I do it, but *how* do I do it?"

"You ask the most difficult questions, Lobsang!" laughed my Guide. "The simplest things are the most difficult to explain. Tell me, how would you explain the process of breathing? You do it, everyone does it, but how does one explain the process?" I nodded glumly. I knew I was always asking questions, but that was the only way to get to know things. Most of the other chelas were not interested, as long as they had their food and not too much work they were satisfied. I wanted more, I wanted to *know*.

"The brain," said the Lama, "is like a radio set, like the device which that man Marconi is using to send messages across the oceans. The collection of particles and electrical charges which constitutes a human being, has the electrical, or radio, device of the brain to tell it what to do. When a person thinks of moving a limb, electric currents race out along the appropriate nerves to galvanise the muscles into the desired action. In the same way, when a person thinks, radio or electrical waves—actually they come from the higher part of the radio spectrum—are radiated from the brain. Certain instruments can detect the radiations and can even chart them into what the Western doctors term 'alpha, beta, delta, and gamma lines.'" I nodded slowly, I had already heard of such things from the Medical Lamas.

"Now," my Guide continued, "sensitive persons can detect these radiations also, and can understand them. I read your thoughts, and when you try, you can read mine. The more two people are in sympathy, in harmony, with each other, the easier it is for them to read these brain radiations which are thoughts. So we get telepathy. Twins are often quite telepathic to each other. Identical twins, where the brain of one is a replica of the other, are so telepathic each to the other that it is often difficult indeed to determine which one originated a thought."

"Respected Sir," I said, "as you know, I can read most minds. Why is this? Are there many more with this particular ability?" "You, Lobsang," replied my Guide, "are especially gifted and specially trained. Your powers are being increased by every method at our command, for you have a difficult task in the Life ahead of you." He shook his head solemnly, "A difficult task indeed. In the Old Days, Lobsang, Mankind could commune telepathically with the animal world. In the years to come, after Mankind has seen the folly of wars, the power will be regained; once again Man and Animal will walk in peace together, neither desiring to harm the other."

Below us a gong boomed and boomed again. There

came the blare of trumpets, and the Lama Mingyar Dondup jumped to his feet, saying, "We must hurry, Lobsang, the Temple Service is about to commence, and His Holiness Himself will be there." I hastily rose to my feet, re-arranged my robe, and rushed after my Guide, now far down the corridor and almost out of sight.

CHAPTER TWO

The great Temple seemed to be a living thing. From my vantage point, high in the roof, I could look down and see the whole vast extent of the place. Earlier in the day my Guide, the Lama Mingyar Dondup, and I had journeyed to this place on a special mission. Now the Lama was closeted with a high dignitary, and I—free to wander—had found this priestly observation post amid the mighty rafters which supported the roof. Prowling about on the walkway of the roof, I had discovered the door and daringly pushed it open. No loud shout of wrath greeting the action, I peeped inside. The place was empty, so I entered and found myself in a small stone room, like a cell built into the stone of the Temple wall. Behind me was the small wooden door, stone walls on either side, and before me a stone ledge perhaps three feet high.

Silently I moved forward and knelt so that only my head was above the stone ledge. I felt like a God in the Heavens peering down on the lowly mortals, peering down on the dim obscurity of the Temple floor so many many feet below. Outside the Temple the purple dusk was giving way to darkness. The last rays of the sinking Sun would be fading behind the snow covered peaks, sending iridescent showers of light through the perpetual spume of snow flying from the very highest ranges.

The darkness of the Temple was relieved, and in places intensified, by hundreds of flickering butter lamps. Lamps which shone as golden points of light, yet still diffused a radiance around. It looked as if the stars were at my feet instead of over my head. Weird shadows stole silently across mighty pillars; shadows now thin and elongated,

25

now short and squat, but always grotesque and bizarre with the cross lighting making the usual seem unearthly, and the unusual strange beyond description.

I peered, staring down, feeling as if in a half-world, uncertain of what I was seeing and what I was imagining. Between me and the floor floated clouds of blue incense smoke rising in layer after layer, reminding me even more of a viewpoint of a God looking down through the clouds of the Earth. Gently rising clouds of incense swirled thickly from the Censers swung by young and devout chelas. Up and down they paced, silent of foot and immobile of face. As they turned and turned again, a million points of light reflected from the golden Censers and sent forth dazzling beams of light. From my vantage I could look down and see the red-glowing incense as, fanned by the breeze, it at times almost flared into flames and sent off showers of red, fast dying sparks. Given fresh life, the incense smoke rose in thicker columns of blue to form trailing paths above and behind the chelas. Rising higher, the smoke formed yet another cloud within the Temple. Wreathing and twisting on the faint air currents from moving monks, it seemed like a thing alive, like a creature, dimly seen, breathing and turning in sleep. For a while I gazed, becoming almost hypnotised with the fantasy that I was inside a living creature, watching the lift and sway of its organs, listening to the sounds of the body, of Life itself.

Through the gloom, through the clouds of incense smoke, I could see the serried ranks of lamas, trappas, and chelas. Sitting cross legged upon the floor they stretched in their endless rows until they became invisible in the farthest recesses of the Temple. All in their Robes of Order they appeared as a living, rippling patch-work of familiar colour. Gold, saffron, red, brown, and a very faint sprinkling of grey, the colours seemed to come alive and flow into each other as their wearers moved. At the head of the Temple sat His Holiness, the Inmost One, the Thirteenth Incarnation of the Dalai Lama, the most revered Figure in the whole of the Buddhist world.

26

For a time I watched, listened to the chant of the deep-voiced lamas accented by the high treble of the small chelas. Watched the incense clouds vibrate in sympathy with the deeper vibrations. Lights flickered into darkness and were replaced, incense burned low and was replenished in a shower of red sparks. The service droned on and I knelt there and watched. Watched the dancing shadows grow and die upon the walls, watched the glittering pin-points of light until I hardly knew where I was or what I was doing.

An aged lama, bent under the weight of years far beyond the normal span, moved slowly before his Brothers of the Order. Around him hovered attentive trappas, with sticks of incense and a light at hand. Bowing to the Inmost One, and turning slowly to bow to each of the Four Corners of the Earth, he at last faced the assembly of monks within the Temple. In a surprisingly strong voice for so aged a man, he chanted:

"Hear the Voices of our Souls. This is the World of Illusion, Life on Earth is but a dream that, in the time of the Life Eternal, is but the twinkling of an eye. Hear the Voices of our Souls, all you that are sore depressed. This Life of Shadow and Sorrow will end, and the Glory of the Life Eternal will shine forth on the righteous. The first stick of incense is lit that a troubled Soul may be guided."

A trappa stood forth and bowed to the Inmost One before turning slowly and bowing in turn to the Four Corners of the Earth. Lighting a stick of incense, he turned again and pointed with it to the Four Corners. The deep-voiced chant rose again and died, to be followed by the high treble of the young chelas. A portly lama recited certain Passages, punctuating them by ringing his Silver Bell with a vigour occasioned only by the presence of the Inmost One. Subsiding into silence, he looked covertly around to see if his performance had obtained due approval.

The Aged Lama stepped forward once more, and bowed to the Inmost One and to the Stations. Another trappa hovered at ready attention, over-anxious in the Presence of the Head of the State and Religion. The aged Lama chanted:

"Hear the Voices of our Souls. This is the World of Illusion. Life on Earth is the Testing, that we may be purified of our dross and soar ever upwards. Hear the Voices of our Souls, all you that are in doubt. Soon the memory of the Earth life will pass away, and there will be Peace, and release from Suffering. The second stick of incense is lit that a doubting Soul may be guided."

The chanting of the monks below me increased and swelled again as the trappa lit the second stick and went through the ritual of bowing to the Inmost One and pointing the incense to each Corner in turn. The walls of the Temple appeared to breathe, to sway in unison with the chanting. Around the Aged Lama ghostly forms gathered, those who had recently passed from this life without the preparation, and who now wandered unguided, and alone.

The flickering shadows seemed to leap and writhe like souls in torment; my own consciousness, my perceptions, my feelings even, flickered between two worlds. In the one I peered with rapt attention at the progress of the Service beneath me. In the other I saw the "between worlds" where the souls of the newly departed trembled in fear at the strangeness of the Unknown. Isolated souls, clad in dank, clinging darkness, they wailed in their terror and loneliness. Apart from each other, apart from all others because of their lack of belief, they were as immobile as a yak stuck in a mountain bog. Into the sticky darkness of the "between worlds," relieved only by the faint blue light from those ghostly forms, came the chanting, the Invitation, of the Aged Lama:

"Hear the Voices of our Souls. This is the World of Illusion. As Man died in the Greater Reality that he might be born on Earth, so must he die on Earth that he may be reborn again to the Greater Reality. There is no Death, but Birth. The pangs of Death are the pangs of Birth. The

28

thick stick of incense is lit that a Soul in Torment may be guided."

Into my consciousness came a telepathic command; "Lobsang! Where are you? Come to me now!" Jerking myself back to *this* world by a great effort. I staggered to my numb feet and tottered out of the little door. "I am coming, Respected Sir!" I thought to my Guide. Rubbing my eyes, watering in the cold night air after the warmth and incense smoke of the Temple, I stumbled and felt my way along high above the ground to where my Guide was waiting in a room right over the main entrance. He smiled as he saw me. "My! Lobsang!" he exclaimed, "you look as if you have seen a ghost!" "Sir!" I replied, "I have seen several."

"Tonight, Lobsang, we shall remain here," said the Lama. "Tomorrow we shall go and call upon the State Oracle. You should find the experience of interest; but now it is time, first for food, and then for sleep. . . ." While we ate I was preoccupied, thinking of what I had seen in the Temple, wondering *how* this was "the World of Illusion." Quickly I finished my supper and went to the room allotted to me. Wrapping myself in my robe, I lay down and soon was fast asleep. Dreams, nightmares, and strange impressions plagued me throughout the night.

I dreamed that I was sitting up, wide awake, and great globes of *something* came at me like the dust in a storm. I was sitting up, and from the great distance small specks appeared, growing larger and larger until I could see that the globes, as they were now, were of all colours. Growing to the size of a man's head, they rushed at me and streaked away beyond. In my dream—if it was a dream!—I could not turn my head to see where they had gone; there were just these endless globes pouring out of nowhere and rushing on past me to—nowhere? It amazed me immensely that none of the globes crashed into me. They looked solid, yet to me they had no substance. With such horrid suddenness that it shook me wide awake, a voice behind me said, "As a ghost sees the stout, solid walls of the

Temple, so now do you!" I shivered in apprehension; was I *dead*? Had I died in the night? But why was I worrying about "death"? I knew that so-called death was merely re-birth. I lay down and eventually fell asleep once more.

The whole world was shaking, creaking, and tumbling in a crazy manner. I sat up in great alarm, thinking that the Temple was falling about me. The night was dark, with only the ghostly radiance of the stars above to shed the merest suspicion of light. Gazing straight ahead of me, I felt my hair rise in fright. I was paralysed; I could not move a finger and worse—the world was growing larger. The smooth stone of the walls coarsened and became porous rock from the extinct volcanoes. The holes in the stone grew and grew and I saw that they were peopled with nightmare creatures which I had seen through the Lama Mingyar Dondup's good German microscope.

The world grew and grew, the frightening creatures grew to ponderous size, becoming so vast with the passage of time that I could see *their* pores! Larger and larger grew the world, then it dawned on me that I was becoming smaller and smaller. I became aware that a dust storm was blowing. From somewhere behind me, the grains of dust roared by, yet none of them touched me. Rapidly they grew larger and larger. Some of them were as large as a man's head, others were as large as the Himalayas. Yet not one touched me. Still they grew larger until I lost all sense of size, until I lost all sense of time. In my dream I appeared to be lying out among the stars, lying cold and motionless while galaxy after galaxy streaked past me and vanished into the distance. How long I remained thus I cannot say. It seemed as if I lay there throughout eternity. At long long last a whole galaxy, a whole series of Universes swung down directly upon me. "This is the end!" I thought vaguely as that multitude of worlds crashed into me.

"Lobsang! Lobsang! Have you gone to the Heavenly Fields?" The Voice boomed and re-echoed around the universe, rebounding from worlds . . . re-echoing from the walls of my stone chamber. Painfully I opened my eyes and tried to get them into focus. Above me was a cluster of bright stars which somehow seemed familiar. Stars which slowly vanished to be replaced by the benign face of the Lama Mingyar Dondup. Gently he was shaking me. Bright sunlight streamed into the room. A sunbeam illuminated some dust motes, and they flashed with all the colours of the rainbow.

"Lobsang! The morning is far advanced. I have let you sleep but now it is time for you to eat and then we will be upon our way." Wearily I scrambled to my feet. I was "out of sorts" this morning; my head seemed to be too big for me, and my mind was still dwelling upon the 'dreams' of the night. Bundling my scant possessions into the front of my robe, I left the room in search of tsampa, our staple food. Down the notched ladder I went, hanging on grimly for fear of falling. Down to where the cook-monks were lounging about.

"I have come for food," I said meekly. "Food? At this time of the morning? Be off with you!" roared the head cook-monk. Reaching out, he was about to give me a blow when another monk whispered hoarsely, "He is with the Lama Mingyar Dondup!" The head cook-monk jumped as if he had been stung by a hornet then bellowed to his assistant, "Well? What are you waiting for? Give the young gentleman his breakfast!" Normally I should have had enough barley in the leather pouch which *all* monks carry, but as we were visiting my supplies were exhausted. All monks, no matter whether chelas, trappas or lamas, carried the leather bag of barley and the bowl from which to eat it. Tsampa was mixed with buttered tea and thus provided the staple food of Tibet. If Tibetan lamaseries printed menus, there would be one word only to print; tsampa!

Somewhat refreshed after my meal, I joined the Lama Mingyar Dondup and we set off on horseback for the Lamasery of the State Oracle. We did not talk while journeying, my horse had a peculiar motion which required my full attention if I were to remain in place. As we travelled along the Lingkor Road, pilgrims, seeing the high rank of my Guide's robes, called to him for blessing. Receiving it, they continued the Holy Circuit looking as if they were at least half way to salvation. Soon we walked our horses through the Willow Grove and came to the stony path leading to the Home of the Oracle. In the court-yard monk-servants took our horses as thankfully I at last slid to the ground.

The place was crowded. The highest lamas had travelled the length and breadth of our country to be present. The Oracle was going to get in communication with the Powers that ruled the world. I, by special arrangement, by special command of the Inmost One, was to be present. We were shown to where we would sleep, I next to the Lama Ming-yar Dondup, and not in a dormitory with many other chelas. As we passed a small temple within the main build-ing, I heard "Hear the Voices of our Souls. This is the World of Illusion."

"Sir!" I said to my Guide when we were alone, *"how* is this the 'World of Illusion'?" He looked at me with a smile. "Well," he replied, "What *is* real? You touch this wall and your finger is stopped by the stone. Therefore you reason that the wall exists as a solid that nothing can penetrate. Beyond the windows the mountain ranges of the Himalayas stand firm as the backbone of the Earth. Yet a ghost, or you in the astral can move as freely through the stone of the mountains as you can through the air." "But how is that 'illusion'?" I asked. "I had a dream last night which really *was* illusion; I feel pale even to think of it!" My Guide, with infinite patience, listened while I told of that dream and when I had finished my tale he said, "I shall have to tell you about the World of Illusion. Not for the moment, though, as we must first call upon the Oracle."

The State Oracle was a surprisingly young man, thin, and of very sickly appearance. I was presented to him and his staring eyes burned straight through me, making tingles

32

of fright race up and down my spine. "Yes! You are the one, I recognise you well," he said. "You have the power within; you shall have the knowledge also. I will see you later." The Lama Mingyar Dondup, my beloved friend, looked well pleased with me. "You pass every test, Lobsang, every time!" he said. "Now come, we will retire to the Sanctuary of the Gods and talk." He smiled down at me as we walked along. "Talk, Lobsang," he remarked, "about the World of Illusion."

The Sanctuary was deserted, as my Guide knew in advance. Flickering lamps burned before the Sacred Images, causing their shadows to jump and move as though in some exotic dance. Incense smoke spiralled upwards to form a low-lying cloud above us. Together we sat by the side of the Lectern from whence the Reader would read from the Sacred Books. We sat in the attitude of contemplation, legs crossed, and fingers entwined.

"This is the World of Illusion," said my Guide, "Wherefore we call to *souls* to hear us, for they alone are in the World of Reality. We say, as you well know, Hear the Voices of our Souls, we do not say Hear our Physical Voices. Listen to me, and do not interrupt, for this is the basis of our Inner Belief. As I shall explain later, people not sufficiently evolved must first have a belief which sustains them, makes them feel that a benevolent Father or Mother is watching over them. Only when one has evolved to the appropriate stage can one accept this which I shall now tell you." I gazed at my Guide, thinking that he was the whole world to me, wishing we could be always together.

"We are creatures of the Spirit," he said, "we are like electric charges endowed with intelligence. This world, this life, is Hell, it is the testing place wherein our Spirit is purified by the suffering of learning to control our gross flesh body. Just as a puppet is controlled by strings manipulated by the Puppet Master, so is our flesh body controlled by strings of electric force from our Overself, our Spirit. A good Puppet Master can create the illusion that the wooden

33

puppets are alive, that they act of their own volition. In the same way *we*, until we learn better, consider that our flesh body is the only thing that matters. In the spirit-strangling atmosphere of the Earth we forget the Soul that truly controls us, we think that we do things of our own free will and are answerable only to our 'conscience.' So, Lobsang, we have the first Illusion, the illusion that the puppet, the flesh body, is the one that matters." He stopped at the sight of my puzzled expression. "Well?" he asked, "and what troubles you?"

"Sir!" I said, "where are my strings of electric force? I cannot see anything connecting me to my Overself!" He laughed as he replied, "Can you see air, Lobsang? Not while you are in the flesh body." Leaning forward he grasped my robe, nearly scaring the life out of me as I stared into his penetrating eyes. "Lobsang!" he said sternly, "have *all* your brains evaporated? Are you *really* bone from the neck up? Have you forgotten the Silver Cord, that collection of lines of electric force linking you— here—with your soul? Truly, Lobsang, *you* are in the World of Illusion!" I felt my face grow red. *Of course* I knew about the Silver Cord, that cord of bluish light which connects the physical body to the spirit body. Many times, when astral travelling, I had watched the Cord shimmering and pulsing with light and life. It was like the umbilical cord which connects the mother and the new-born child, only the "child" which was the physical body could not exist for a moment if the Silver Cord was severed.

I looked up, my Guide was ready to continue after my interruption. "When we are in the physical world we tend to think that *only* the physical world matters. That is one of the safety devices of the Overself; if we remembered the Spirit World with its happiness we would be able to remain here only by a strong effort of will. If we remembered past lives when, perhaps, we were more important than in this life, we should not have the necessary humility. We will have some tea brought in and then I will show you, or tell you, of the life of a Chinaman from his death,

34

to his rebirth and to his death and arrival in the Next World." The Lama stretched forth his hand to ring the small silver bell in the Sanctuary, then stopped at my expression. "Well?" he asked, "what is your question?" "Sir!" I answered, "why a Chinaman? Why not a Tibetan?" "Because," he replied, "if I say 'a Tibetan' you will try to associate the name with someone you know—with incorrect results." He rang the bell and a servant-monk brought us tea. My Guide looked at me thoughtfully. "Do you realise that in drinking this tea we are swallowing millions of worlds?" he asked. "Fluids have a more sparsely molecular content. If you could magnify the molecules of this tea you would find that they roll like the sands beside a turbulent lake. Even a gas, even the air itself is composed of molecules, of minute particles. However, that is a digression, we were going to discuss the death and life of a Chinaman." He finished his tea and waited while I finished mine.

"Seng was an old mandarin," said my Guide. "His life had been a fortunate one and now, in the evening of that life he felt a great contentment. His family was large, his concubines and slaves many. Even the Emperor of China himself had shown him favours. As his aged eyes peered short-sightedly through the window of his room he could dimly discern the beautiful gardens with the strutting peacocks. Softly to his failing ears came the song of birds returning to the trees as the day grew old. Seng lay back, relaxed upon his cushions. Within himself he could feel the rustling fingers of Death loosing his bonds with life. Slowly the blood red sun sank behind the ancient pagoda. Slowly Old Seng sank back upon his cushions, a harsh rattling breath hissing through his teeth. The sunlight faded, and the little lamps in the room were lighted, but Old Seng had gone, gone with the last dying rays of the sun." My Guide looked at me in order to be sure that I was following him, then continued.

"Old Seng lay slumped upon his cushions, with his body sounds creaking and wheezing into silence. No longer did blood rush through arteries and veins, no longer did body fluids gurgle within. The body of Old Seng was dead, finished with, of no more use. But a clairvoyant, if one had been present, would have seen a light blue haze form around the body of Old Seng. Form, then lift over the body, floating horizontally above, attached by the thinning Silver Cord. Gradually the Silver Cord thinned, and parted. The Soul which had been Old Seng floated off, drifted like a cloud of incense smoke, vanished effortlessly through the walls." The Lama refilled his cup, saw that I also had tea, then continued.

"The Soul drifted on through realms, through dimensions which the materialist mind cannot comprehend. At last he reached a wondrous parkland, dotted with immense buildings at one of which he stopped, here the Soul that had been Old Seng entered and made his way across a gleaming floor. A soul, Lobsang, in its own surroundings, is as solid as you are upon this world. The soul in the world of the soul, can be confined by walls, and walk upon a floor. The soul there has different abilities and talents from those we know upon the Earth. This Soul wandered on and at last entered a small cubicle. Sitting down, he gazed at the wall before him. Suddenly the wall appeared to vanish, and in its place he saw scenes, the scenes of his life. He saw that which we term The Akashic Record, which is the Record of all that has ever happened and which can be seen readily by those who are trained. It is also seen by *everyone* who passes from the Earth life to the life beyond, for Man sees the Record of his own successes and failures. Man sees his past and *judges himself!* There is no sterner judge than Man himself. We do not sit trembling before a God; we sit and see all that we did and all that we meant to do." I sat silent, I found all this of quite absorbing interest. I could listen to this for hours— better than dull lessonwork!

"The Soul that had been Old Seng the Chinese Mandarin sat and saw again the life that he, upon Earth, had thought so successful," continued my Guide. "He saw, and

36

sorrowed for his many faults, and then he rose and left the cubicle, going speedily to a larger room where men and women of the Soul World awaited him. Silently, smiling with compassion and understanding, they awaited his approach, his request to be guided. Sitting in their company he told them of his faults, of the things he had attempted to do, *meant* to do, and failed." "But I thought you said he was not judged, he judged himself!" I said quickly. "That is so, Lobsang," replied my Guide. "Having seen his past and his mistakes, he now approached these Advisors in order to receive their suggestions—but do not interrupt, listen to me and save your questions for after."

"As I was saying," continued the Lama, "the Soul sat with the Advisors and told them of his failures, told them of the qualities which he had to 'grow' in to his Soul before he could evolve further. First would come the return to view his body, then would come a period of rest—years or hundreds of years—and then he would be helped to find conditions such as were essential for his further progress. The Soul that had been Old Seng went back to Earth to gaze finally upon his dead body, now ready for burial. Then, no longer the Soul of Old Seng, but a Soul ready for rest, he returned to the Land Beyond. For a time unspecified he rested and recuperated, studying the lessons of past lives, preparing for the life to come. Here, in this life beyond death, articles and substances were as solid to his touch as they had been on Earth. He rested until the time and conditions were pre-arranged." "I like this!" I exclaimed. "I find it of great interest." My Guide smiled at me before continuing.

"At some pre-determined time, the Soul in Waiting was called and was led forth into the World of Mankind by one whose task was such service. They stopped, invisible to the eyes of those in the flesh, watching the parents-to-be, looking at the house, assessing the probabilities that *this* house would afford the desired facilities for learning the lessons which had to be learned this time. Satisfied, they withdrew. Months later the Mother-to-Be felt a sudden quickening inside her as the Soul entered and the Baby came to life. In time the Baby was born to the World of Man. The Soul that had once activated the body of Old Seng now struggled anew with the reluctant nerves and brain of the child Le Wong living in humble circumstances in a fishing village of China. Once again the high vibrations of a Soul were converted to the lower octave vibrations of a flesh body."

I sat and thought. Then I thought some more. At last I said, "Honourable Lama, as this is so, why do people fear death, which is but a release from the troubles of Earth?" "That is a sensible question, Lobsang," replied my Guide. "Did we but remember the joys of the Other World many of us would not be able to tolerate hardships here, wherefore we have implanted within us a fear of death." Giving me a quizzical sideways glance, he remarked, "Some of us do not like school, do not like the discipline so necessary at school. Yet when one grows up and becomes adult the benefits of school become apparent. It would not do to run away from school and expect to advance in learning; nor is it advisable to end one's life before one's allotted time." I wondered about this, because just a few days before an old monk, illiterate and sick, had thrown himself from a high hermitage. A sour old man he had been, with a disposition that made him refuse all offers of help. Yes, old Jigme was better out of the way, I thought. Better for himself. Better for others.

"Sir!" I said, "then the monk Jigme was at fault when he ended his own life?" "Yes, Lobsang, he was very much at fault," replied my Guide. "A man or woman has a certain allotted span upon the Earth. If one ends his or her life before that time, then he or she has to return almost immediately. Thus we have the spectacle of a baby born to live perhaps a few months only. That will be the soul of a suicide returning to take over the body and so live out the time which should have been lived before. Suicide is *never* justified; it is a grave offence against oneself, against one's Overself." "But Sir," I said, "how about the high born Japanese who commits ceremonial suicide in order to atone for family disgrace? Surely he is a brave man that he does that." "Not so, Lobsang," my Guide was most emphatic. "Not so. Bravery consists not of dying but of living in face of hardship, in face of suffering. To die is easy, to live—*that* is the brave act! Not even the theatrical demonstration of pride in 'Ceremonial Suicide' can blind one to its wrongness. We are here to learn and we can only learn through living our allotted span. Suicide is *never* justified!" I thought again of old Jigme. He was very old when he killed himself, so when he came again, I thought, it would be for a short stay only.

"Honourable Lama," I asked, "what is the purpose of fear? Why do we have to suffer so much through fear? Already I have discovered that the things I fear most never happen, yet I fear them still!" The Lama laughed and said, "That happens to us all. We fear the Unknown. Yet fear is necessary. Fear spurs us on when otherwise we should be slothful. Fear gives us added strength with which to avoid accidents. Fear is a booster which gives us added power, added incentive, and makes us overcome our own inclination to laziness. You would not study your school work unless you *feared* the teacher or *feared* appearing stupid in front of others."

Monks were coming into the Sanctuary; chelas darted around lighting more butter lamps, more incense. We rose to our feet and walked out into the cool of the evening where a slight breeze played with the leaves of the willows. The great trumpets sounded from the Potala so far away, and dimly the echoes rolled around the walls of the State Oracle Lamasery.

CHAPTER THREE

The Lamasery of the State Oracle was small, compact, and very secluded. Few small chelas played with carefree abandon. No groups of trappas lounged indolently in the sun-drenched courtyard, whiling away the noonday hour in idle chatter. Old men—old Lamas too!—were in the majority here. Aged men, white of hair and bent under the weight of years, they went slowly about their business. This was the Home of the Seers. To the aged lamas in general, and to the Oracle himself, was entrusted the task of Prophecy, of Divination. No uninvited visitor entered here, no stray traveller called in search of rest or food. This was a place feared by many and forbidden to all except those specially invited. My Guide, the Lama Mingyar Dondup was the exception; at any time he could enter and find that he was indeed a welcome visitor.

A gracious grove of trees gave the Lamasery privacy from prying eyes. Strong stone walls gave the buildings protection from the over-curious, if there should be any who would risk the wrath of the powerful Oracle Lama for idle curiosity. Carefully kept rooms were set aside for His Holiness the Inmost One who so frequently visited this Temple of Knowledge. The air was quiet, the general impression was of quietude, of men placidly going about their important business.

Nor was there opportunity for brawls, for noisy intruders. The Place was patrolled by the mighty Men of Kham, the huge men, many of them over seven feet tall, and none of them weighing less than two hundred and fifty pounds, who were employed throughout Tibet as monk-police charged with the task of keeping order in communities of sometimes thousands of monks. The monk-police strode about the grounds constantly alert, constantly on guard. Carrying mighty staves they were indeed a frightening sight to those with guilty consciences. A monk's robe does not necessarily cover a religious man; there are wrong-doers and lazy men in all communities, so the Men of Kham were busy.

The lamastic buildings too were in keeping with their intended purpose. No high buildings here, no long notched poles to scale; this was for aged men, men who had lost the elasticity of youth, men whose bones were frail. The corridors were easy of access, and those of greatest age lived upon the ground floor. The State Oracle himself also lived upon the ground floor, at the side of the Temple of Divination. Around him lodged the oldest men, the most learned. And the senior monk-police of the Men of Kham.

"We will go to see the Oracle, Lobsang," said my Guide. "He has expressed great interest in you and is prepared to give you much of his time." The invitation——or command ——filled me with the greatest gloom; any visit to an astrol-oger or 'seer' in the past had been productive of *bad* news, more suffering, more confirmation of hardships to come. Usually, too, I had to wear my best robe and sit like a stuffed duck while listening to some prosy old man bleat-ing out a string of platitudes which I would rather not hear. I looked up suspiciously; the Lama was struggling to conceal a smile as he gazed down at me. Obviously, I thought dourly, he had been reading my mind! He broke into a laugh as he said, "Go as you are, the Oracle is not at all swayed by the state of one's robe. He knows more about you than you know yourself!" My gloom deepened, what *was* I going to hear next, I wondered.

We walked down the corridor and went out into the inner courtyard. I glanced at the looming mountain ranges, feeling like one going to execution. A scowling police-monk approached, looking to me almost like a mountain on the move. Recognising my Guide he broke into welcoming smiles and bowed deeply. "Prostrations at thy Lotus Feet,

41

Holy Lama," he said. "Honour me by permitting me to lead you to His Reverence the State Oracle." He fell into step beside us and I felt sure that the ground trembled to his ponderous tread.

Two lamas stood beside the door, lamas, not ordinary monk-guards, at our approach they stood aside that we might enter. "The Holy One awaits you," said one smiling upon my Guide. "He is looking forward to your visit, Lord Mingyar," said the other. We walked in and found ourselves to be in a somewhat dimly lighted room. For some seconds I could distinguish very little indeed; my eyes had been dazzled by the bright sunlight in the courtyard. Gradually, as my vision returned to normal, I perceived a bare room with but two tapestries upon the walls and a small incense burner which stood smoking in a corner. In the centre of the room, upon a plain cushion, sat a quite young man. He looked thin and frail, and I was amazed indeed when I realised that *this* was the State Oracle of Tibet. His eyes protruded somewhat, and stared at me and through me. I had the impression that he was seeing my soul and not my earthly body.

My Guide, the Lama Mingyar Dondup, and I prostrated ourselves in traditional and prescribed greeting, then we rose to our feet and stood waiting. At last, when the silence was becoming decidedly uncomfortable, the Oracle spoke. "Welcome, Lord Mingyar, welcome Lobsang!" he said. His voice was somewhat high in pitch and was not at all strong; it gave the impression of coming from a great distance. For a few moments my Guide and the Oracle discussed matters of common interest, then the Lama Mingyar Dondup bowed, turned, and left the room. The Oracle sat looking at me and at last said, "Bring a cushion and sit by me, Lobsang." I reached for one of the padded squares resting against a far wall and placed it so that I could sit before him. For a time he gazed at me in a somewhat moody silence, but at long last, when I was becoming uncomfortable beneath his scrutiny, he spoke. "So you are Tuesday Lobsang Rampa!" he said. "We knew each other

42

well in another phase of existence. Now, by order of the Inmost One, I have to tell you of hardships to come, difficulties to overcome." "Oh, Sir!" I exclaimed, "I must have done terrible things in past lives to have to suffer thus in this. My Karma, my predestined Fate, seems to be harder than anyone else's." "Not so," he replied, "it is a very common mistake for people to think that because they have hardships in *this* life they are necessarily suffering for the sins of past lives. If you heat metal in a furnace do you do so because the metal has erred and must be punished, or do you do it in order to *improve* the qualities of the material?" He looked hard at me and said, "However, your Guide the Lama Mingyar Dondup will discuss that with you. I have to tell you only of the future."

The Oracle touched a silver bell and an attendant entered silently. Padding across to us he placed a very low table between the State Oracle and me, and upon the table he placed an ornate silver bowl lined, apparently, with a form of porcelain. Within the bowl glowed charcoal embers which flared bright red as the monk-attendant swung it in the air before placing it in front of the Oracle. With a muttered word, the import of which was lost upon me, he placed a richly carved wooden box to the right of the bowl, and departed as silently as he had come. I sat still, ill at ease, wondering why all this had to happen to me. *Everyone* was telling me what a hard life I was going to have; they seemed to delight in it. Hardship was hardship, even though apparently I was not having to pay for the sins of some past life. Slowly the Oracle reached forward and opened the box. With a small gold spoon he ladled out a fine powder which he sprinkled on to the glowing embers.

The room filled with a fine blue haze; I felt my senses reel and my sight grow dim. From a measureless distance away I seemed to hear the tolling of a great bell. Closer came the sound, and its intensity grew and grew until I felt my head would split. My sight cleared and I watched intently as a column of smoke rose endlessly from the bowl. Within the smoke I saw movement, movement which

43

came closer and engulfed me so that I was part of it. From somewhere beyond my comprehension the voice of the State Oracle reached me, droning on and on. But I had no need of his voice, I was *seeing* the future, seeing it as vividly as he. Within a point of Time I stood apart and watched the events of my life reel before me as if pictured upon an ever-moving film. My early childhood, events in my life, the fierceness of my father—all were portrayed before me. Once again I sat before the great Lamasery of Chakpori. Once again I felt the hard rocks of the Iron Mountain as the wind whipped me from the Lamasery roof to fling me with bone-breaking force down the mountain side. The smoke swirled and the pictures (what we term "the Akashic Record") moved on. I saw again my initiation, secret ceremonies wreathed in smoke as I was not then initiated. On the pictures I saw myself setting out on the long, lonely trail to Chungking in China.

A strange machine twisted and tossed in the air, soaring and falling above the steep cliffs of Chungking. And I—I—was at the controls! Later I saw fleets of such machines, with the Rising Sun of Japan flaunted from their wings. From the machines fell black blobs which rushed to the earth to erupt into flame and smoke. Wrecked bodies hurtled heaven-wards, and for a time the skies rained blood and human fragments. I felt sick at heart, and dazed, as the pictures moved and showed me myself being tortured by the Japanese. I saw my life, saw the hardships, felt the bitterness. But the greatest sorrow of all was the treachery and evil of some people of the Western world, who, I saw, were bent on destroying work for good for the sole reason that they were jealous. The pictures moved on and on, and I saw the probable course of my life before I lived it.

As I well knew, *probabilities* can be most accurately forecast. Only the minor details are sometimes different. One's astrological configurations set the limit of what one can be and can endure just as the governor of an engine can set its minimum and maximum speeds. "A hard life for me, all right!" I thought. Then I jumped so hard that I almost left the cushion; a hand was laid upon my shoulder. As I turned I saw the face of the State Oracle, now sitting behind me. His look was of utter compassion, of sorrow for the difficult way ahead. "You are very psychic, Lobsang," he said, "I normally have to explain these pictures to onlookers. The Inmost One, as one would expect, is quite correct."

"All I want," I replied, "is to stay here in peace. Why should I want to go to the Western world where they so ardently preach religion—and try to cut one's throat behind one's back?" "There is a Task, my friend," said the Oracle, "which *must* be accomplished. *You* can do it in spite of all oppositions. Hence the special and difficult training which you are undergoing." It made me feel most glum, all this talk about hardships and Tasks. All I wanted was peace and quiet and some harmless amusement now and then. "Now," said the Oracle, "it is time for you to return to your Guide, for he has much to tell you and he is expecting you." I rose to my feet and bowed before turning and leaving the room. Outside the huge monk-policeman was waiting to lead me to the Lama Mingyar Dondup. Together we walked, side by side, and I thought of a picture book I had seen wherein an elephant and an ant walked a jungle path side by side. . . .

"Well, Lobsang!" said the Lama as I entered his room. "I hope you are not too depressed at all that you have seen?" He smiled at me and motioned for me to sit. "Food for the body first, Lobsang, and then food for the Soul," he exclaimed laughingly as he rang his silver bell for the monk-attendant to bring our tea. Evidently I had arrived just in time! Lamasery rules stated that one must not look about while one was eating, one's eyes should not stray, and full attention should be given to the Voice of the Reader. Here in the Lama Mingyar Dondup's room there was no Reader perched high above us, reading aloud from the Sacred Books in order to keep our thoughts from such common things as food. Nor were there any stern Proctors ready to jump at us for the slightest infraction of the Rules. I gazed out of the window at the Himalayas stretching endlessly before me, thinking that soon the time would come when I should gaze upon them no more. I had received glimpses into the future—*my* future—and I dreaded the things which I had not seen clearly but which had been partly veiled in smoke.

"Lobsang!" said my Guide, "you have seen much, but much more has remained hidden. If you feel that you cannot face the planned Future, then we will accept the fact—though sadly—and you may remain in Tibet." "Sir!" I replied, "you once told me that the man who sets out upon one of Life's Paths, falters, and turns back, is no man. I will go ahead in spite of knowing the difficulties before me." He smiled, and nodded his approval. "As I expected," he said, "you will succeed in the end." "Sir!" I asked, "why do not people come to this world with a knowledge of what they have been in past lives and what they are supposed to do in this life? Why must there be what you term 'Hidden Knowledge'? Why cannot we all know everything?"

The Lama Mingyar Dondup raised his eyebrows and laughed. "You certainly want to know a lot!" he said. "Your memory is failing, too, quite recently I told you that we do not normally remember our past lives as to do so would be to increase our load upon this world. As we say, 'The Wheel of Life revolves, bringing riches to one and poverty to another. The beggar of today is the prince of tomorrow.' If we do not know of our past lives we all start afresh without trying to trade on what we were in our last incarnation." "But," I asked, "what about the Hidden Knowledge? If all people had that knowledge everyone would be better, would advance more quickly." My Guide smiled down at me. "It is not so simple as that!" he replied. For a moment he sat in silence, then he spoke again.

"There are powers within us, within the control of our Overself, immeasurably greater than anything that Man has been able to make in the material, the physical world. Western Man in particular would abuse such Powers as we can command, for all that Western Man cares about is money. Western Man has but two questions: can you prove it? and—what do I get out of it?" He laughed quite boyishly and said, "I always feel most amused when I think of the vast array of mechanisms and apparatus which Man uses to send a 'wireless' message across the oceans. 'Wireless' is the last term they should use, for the apparatus consists of miles and miles of wire. But here, in Tibet, our trained lamas send telepathic messages with no apparatus at all. We go into the astral and travel through space and time, visiting other parts of the world, and other worlds. We can levitate—lift immense loads by the application of powers not generally known. Not all men are pure, Lobsang, nor does a monk's robe always cover a holy man. There can be an evil man in a lamasery just as there can be a saint in prison." I looked at him in some puzzlement. "But if all men had this knowledge, surely they would all be good?" I asked.

The Lama looked at me sorrowfully as he replied. "We keep the Secret Knowledge *secret* in order that Mankind may be safeguarded. Many men, particularly those of the West, think only of money and of power over others. As has been foretold by the Oracle and others, this our land will later be invaded and physically conquered by a strange cult, a cult which has no thought for the common man, but exists solely in order to bolster up the power of dictators, dictators who will enslave half the world. There have been high lamas who have been tortured to death by the Russians because the lamas would not divulge forbidden knowledge. The average man, Lobsang, who suddenly had access to forbidden knowledge, would react like this: first he would be fearful of the power now within his grasp. Then it would occur to him that he had the means of making himself rich beyond his wildest dreams. He would experiment, and money would come to him. With increasing money and power he would desire yet more money and power. A millionaire is never satisfied with one million, but wants many millions more! It is said that in the unevolved, absolute power corrupts. The Hidden Knowledge gives absolute power."

A great light dawned upon me; I knew how Tibet could be saved! Jumping up excitedly, I exclaimed, "Then Tibet is saved! The Hidden Knowledge will save us from invasion!" My Guide looked upon me with compassion. "No, Lobsang," he replied sadly, "we do not use the Powers for things like that. Tibet will be persecuted, almost annihilated, but in the years to come she will rise again and become greater, purer. The country will be purified of dross in the furnace of war just as, later, the whole world will be." He gave me a sideways glance. "There *have* to be wars, you know, Lobsang!" he said quietly. "If there were no wars the population of the world would become too great. If there were no wars there would be plagues. Wars and sickness regulate the population of the world and provide opportunities for people on the Earth—and on other worlds—to do good to others. There will *always* be wars until the population of the world can be controlled in some other way."

The gongs were summoning us to the evening service. My Guide the Lama Mingyar Dondup rose to his feet. "Come along, Lobsang," he said, "we are guests here and must show respect for our hosts by attending the service." We walked out of the room and went into the courtyard. The gongs were calling insistently—being sounded longer than would have been the case at Chakpori. We made our surprisingly slow way to the Temple. I wondered at our slowness, then as I looked around I saw very aged men, and the infirm, hobbling across the courtyard in our footsteps. My Guide whispered to me, "It would be a courtesy, Lobsang, if you went across and sat with those chelas!" Nodding, I made my way round the inner walls of the Temple until I came to where the chelas of the State Oracle Lamasery were sitting. They eyed me with curiosity as I sat down to one side of them. Almost imperceptibly, when the Proctors were not looking, they edged forward until they surrounded me.

"Where do you come from?" asked one boy, who seemed to be the leader. "Chakpori," I replied in a whisper. "You the fellow sent by the Inmost One?" whispered another. "Yes," I whispered back, "I have been to see the Oracle, he told me——" "SILENCE!" roared a fierce voice just behind me, "Not another sound out of you boys!" I saw the big man move away. "Ga!" said a boy, "don't take any notice of him, his bark is worse than his bite." Just then the State Oracle and an Abbot appeared through a small door at the side, and the service commenced.

Soon we were streaming out into the open again. With the others I went to the kitchen to have my leather barley bag refilled and to get tea. There was no opportunity to talk; monks of all degree were standing about, having a last minute discussion before retiring for the night. I made my way to the room allotted to me, rolled myself in my robe and lay down to sleep. Sleep did not come quickly, though. I gazed out at the purple darkness, pinpointed by the golden-flamed butter lamps. Far away the eternal Himalayas stretched rock-fingers skywards as if in supplication to the Gods of the World. Vivid white shafts of moonlight flashed through mountain crevices, to disappear and flash again as the moon climbed higher. There was no breeze tonight, the prayer flags hung listlessly from their poles. The merest trace of cloud floated indolently above the City of Lhasa. I turned over, and fell into a dreamless sleep.

In the very early hours of the morning I awakened with a start of fright; I had overslept and would be late for the early service. Jumping to my feet, I hastily shrugged into my robe and bolted for the door. Racing down the deserted corridor I dashed out into the courtyard—straight into the arms of one of the Men of Kham. "Where are you going?" he whispered fiercely as he held me in an iron grip. "To early morning service," I replied,

"I must have overslept." He laughed and released me. "Oh!" he said, "you are a visitor. There is no early service here. Go back and sleep again." "No early service?" I cried, "why, *everyone* has early service!" The monk-policeman must have been in a good mood, for he answered me civilly, "We have old men here, and some who are infirm, for that reason we dispense with the early service. Go, and rest awhile in peace." He patted me on the head, gently for him, like a thunderclap for me, and pushed me back into the corridor. Turning, he resumed his pacing of the courtyard, his ponderous footsteps going "bonk! bonk!" with the heavy stave going "thunk! thunk!" as the butt thudded into the ground at every other step. I raced back along the corridor and in minutes was sound asleep again.

Later in the day I was presented to the Abbot and two of the senior lamas. They questioned me intently, asking me questions about my home life, what I remembered of past lives, my relationship with my Guide, the Lama Mingyar Dondup. Finally the three rose totteringly to their feet and filed toward the door. "Come" said the last one, crooking a finger in my direction. Dumbfounded, walking as one in a daze, I followed meekly behind. They wended a slow way out of the door and shuffled lethargically along the corridor. I followed, almost tripping over my feet in an effort to go slowly enough. We crawled on, past open rooms where trappas and chelas alike looked up in curiosity at our slow passing. I felt my cheeks burn with embarrassment at being on the "tail" of this procession; at its head, the Abbot shuffling along with the aid of two sticks. Next came two old lamas who were so decrepit and withered that they could scarce keep up with the Abbot. And I, bringing up the rear, could hardly go slowly enough.

At long last, or it seemed "long last" to me, we reached a small doorway set in a far wall. We stopped while the Abbot fumbled with a key and mumbled beneath his breath. One of the lamas stepped forward to assist him, and eventually a door was pushed open with a squeal of protesting hinges. The Abbot entered, followed by first one lama and then the other. No one said anything to me, so I went in as well. An old lama pushed the door shut behind me. Before me there was a fairly long table laden with old and dust-covered objects. Old robes, ancient Prayer Wheels, old bowls, and assorted strings of Prayer Beads. Scattered on the table were a few Charm Boxes and various other objects which I could not at first glance identify. "Hmmmn. Mmmmn. Come here my boy!" commanded the Abbot. I moved reluctantly toward him and he grasped my left arm with his bony hand. I felt as if in the clutch of a skeleton! "Hmmmn. Mmmmn. Boy! Hmmmn. Which, if any, of these objects and articles were in your possession during a past life?" He led me the length of the table, then turned me about and said, "Hmmmn. Mmmmn. If you believe that any article was yours. Hmmmn, pick it or them out and Hmmmn, Mmmmn, bring it or them to me." He sat down heavily and appeared to take no more interest in my activities. The two lamas sat with him, and no word was uttered.

"Well!" I thought to myself, "if the three old men want to play it this way—all right, I will play it their way!" Psychometry is, of course, the simplest thing of all to do. I walked slowly along with my left hand extended palm down over the various articles. At certain objects I experienced a form of itch in the centre of the palm, and a slight shiver, or tremor, thrilled along my arm. I picked out a Prayer Wheel, an old battered bowl, and a string of beads. Then I repeated my journey by the side of the long table. Only one more article caused my palm to itch and my arm to tingle; an old tattered robe in the last stages of decay. The saffron robe of a high official, the colour almost bleached out by age, the material rotten and powdery to the touch. Gingerly I picked it up, half afraid that it would disintegrate between my cautious hands. Carefully I carried it to the old Abbot, deposited it at his feet, and returned for the Prayer Wheel, the

51

battered bowl, and the string of beads. Without a word the Abbot and the two lamas examined the articles and compared certain signs, or secret markings, with those in an old black book which the Abbot produced. For a time they sat facing each other, heads a-nod on withered necks, ancient brains almost creaking with the effort to think.

"Harrumph! Arrrf!" mumbled the Abbot, wheezing like an over-worked yak. "Mmmmmnnn. It is indeed he. Hmmmn. A remarkable performance. Mmmmn. Go to your Guide, the Lama Mingyar Dondup, my boy, and Hmmmn, tell him that we should be honoured by his presence. You my boy, need not return. Harrumph! Arrrf!" I turned and raced from the room, glad to be free from these living mummies whose dessicated remoteness was so far removed from the warm humanity of the Lama Mingyar Dondup. Scurrying round a corner I came to a full stop inches from my Guide. He laughed at me and said, "Oh! Don't look so startled, I received the message also." Giving me a friendly pat on the back he hastened on toward the room containing the Abbot and the two old lamas. I wandered out into the courtyard and idly kicked a stone or two.

"You the fellow whose Incarnation is being Recognised?" asked a voice behind me. I turned to see a chela regarding me intently. "I don't know what they are doing," I replied. "All I know is that I have been dragged round the corridors so that I could pick out some of my old things. *Anyone* could do that!" The boy laughed good-naturedly, "You Chakpori men know your stuff," he said, "or you would not be in that Lamasery. I heard it said that you were someone *big* in a past life. You *must* have been for the Oracle Himself to devote half a day to you." He shrugged his shoulders in mock horror and remarked, "You'd better look out. Before you know what is happening they will have Recognised you and made you an Abbot. Then you won't be able to play with the other men at Chakpori any longer."

From a door at the far end of the courtyard appeared the form of my Guide. Rapidly he strode toward us. The Chela with whom I had been talking bowed low in humble salutation. The Lama smiled upon him and spoke kindly —as always. "We must be on our way, Lobsang!" said the Lama Mingyar Dondup to me, "soon night will be upon us, and we do not want to ride through the darkness." Together we walked to the stables where a monk-groom was waiting with our horses. Reluctantly I mounted and followed my Guide on to the path through the willow trees. We jogged along in silence; I could never converse intelligently on horse-back as the whole of my energies was devoted to staying on. To my astonishment we did not turn off at Chakpori, but wended our way on to the Potala. Slowly the horses climbed the Road of Steps. Beneath us the Valley was already fading into the shadows of the night. Gladly I dismounted and hurried into the now-familiar Potala in search of food.

My Guide was waiting for me when I went to my room after supper. "Come in with me, Lobsang," he called. I went in and at his bidding seated myself. "Well!" he said, "I expect you are wondering what it is all about." "Oh! I expect to be Recognised as an Incarnation!" I replied airily. "One of the men and I were discussing it at the State Oracle Lamasery when you called me away!" "Well that is very nice for you," said the Lama Mingyar Dondup. "Now we have to take some time and discuss things. You need not attend service tonight. Sit more comfortably and listen, and do not keep interrupting."

"Most people come to this world in order to learn things," commenced my Guide. "Others come in order that they may assist those in need, or to complete some special, highly important task." He looked sharply at me to make sure that I was following, then continued, "Many religions preach about a Hell, the place of punishment, or expiation for one's sins. Hell is *here,* on this world. Our real life is on the other World. Here we come to learn, to pay for mistakes made in previous lives or—as I said

53

—to attempt the accomplishment of some highly important task. You are here to do a task in connection with the human aura. Your 'tools' will be an exceptionally sensitive psychic perception, a greatly intensified ability to see the human aura, and all the knowledge that we can give you concerning *all* the occult arts. The Inmost One has decreed that every possible means be used to increase your abilities and talents. Direct teaching, actual experiences, hypnotism, we are going to use them all in order that we may get the most knowledge into you in the shortest time."

"Hell it is, all right!" I exclaimed gloomily. The Lama laughed at my expression. "But *this* Hell is merely the stepping stone to a far better life," he replied. "Here we are able to get rid of some of the baser faults. Here, in a few years of Earth life, we shed faults which may have plagued us in the Other World for countless spans of time. The whole life of this world is but the twinkling of an eye to that of the Other World. Most people in the West," he went on, "think that when one 'dies' one sits on a cloud and plays a harp. Others think that when one leaves *this* world for the next one they exist in a mystical state of nothingness and like it." He laughed and continued, "If we could only get them to realise that the life after death is *more* real than anything on Earth! Everything on this world consists of vibrations; the whole world's vibrations—and everything within the world—may be likened to an octave on a musical scale. When we pass to the Other Side of Death the 'octave' is raised further up the scale." My Guide stopped, seized my hand and rapped my knuckles on the floor. "That, Lobsang," he said, "is stone, the vibrations which we term stone." Again he took my hand and rubbed my fingers on my robe. "That," he exclaimed, "is the vibration which indicates wool. If we move *everything* up the scale of vibrations we still maintain the relative degrees of hardness and softness. So, in the Life after Death, the *real* Life, we can possess things just as we do on this world. Do you follow that clearly?" he asked.

Obviously it was clear, I had known things like that for a very long time. The Lama broke into my thoughts. "Yes, I am aware that all this is common knowledge here, but if we *vocalize* these 'unspoken thoughts' we shall make it clearer in your mind. Later," he said, "you will journey to the lands of the Western world. There you will meet many difficulties through Western religions." He smiled somewhat wryly and remarked, "The Christians call us heathens. In their Bible it is written that 'Christ wandered in the wilderness.' In *our* records it is revealed that Christ wandered throughout India, studying Indian religions, and then He came to Lhasa and studied at the Jo Kang under our foremost priests of that time. Christ formulated a *good* religion, but the Christianity practised today is not the religion that Christ produced." My Guide looked at me somewhat severely and said, "I know you are a little bored by this, thinking I am talking for the sake of words, but I have travelled throughout the Western world and I have a duty to warn you of what you will experience. I can do that best by telling you of their religions, for I know you have an eidetic memory." I had the grace to blush; I *had* been thinking "too many words!"

Outside in the corridors monks were shush-shushing along toward the Temple to the evening service. On the roof above trumpeters looked out across the Valley and sounded the last notes of the dying day. Here, in front of me, my Guide the Lama Mingyar Dondup continued his talk. "There are two basic religions in the West but innumerable subdivisions. The Jewish religion is old and tolerant. You will have no trouble, no difficulties caused by Jews. For centuries they have been persecuted, and they have great sympathy and understanding for others. The Christians are not so tolerant, except on Sundays. I am not going to say anything about individual beliefs, you

55

will read of them, but I am going to say how religions started.

"In the early days of life upon Earth," said the Lama, "people were first in little groups, very small tribes. There were no laws, no code of behaviour. Strength was the only law; a stronger and fiercer tribe made war upon those weaker. In course of time a stronger and wiser man arose. He realised that his tribe would be the strongest if it were organised. He founded a religion and a code of behaviour. 'Be fruitful and multiply,' he commanded, knowing that the more babies were born the stronger would his tribe grow. 'Honour thy father and thy mother,' he ordered, knowing that if he gave parents authority over their children he would have authority over the parents. Knowing too that if he could persuade children to feel indebted to their parents, discipline would be easier to enforce. 'Thou shalt not commit adultery,' thundered the Prophet of that time. His real command was that the *tribe* should not be 'adulterated' with the blood of a member of another tribe, for in such cases there are divided loyalties. In course of time the priests found that there were some who did not always obey religious teachings. After much thought, much discussion, those priests worked out a scheme of reward and punishment. 'Heaven,' 'Paradise,' 'Valhalla,'—term it what you will—for those who obeyed *the priests*. Hell fire and damnation with everlasting tortures for those who disobeyed."

"Then you are opposed to the organised religions of the West, Sir?" I asked. "No, most certainly not," replied my Guide, "there are many who feel lost unless they can feel or imagine an all-seeing Father peering down at them, with a Recording Angel ready to note any good deeds as well as bad! We are God to the microscopic creatures who inhabit our bodies, and the even smaller creatures that inhabit *his* molecules! As for prayer, Lobsang, do you often listen to the prayers of the creatures existing on your molecules?" "But you said that prayer was effective," I responded with some astonishment. "Yes,

Lobsang, prayer is *very* effective *if we pray to our own overself*, to the real part of us in another world, the part which controls our 'puppet strings'. Prayer is *very* effective *if* we obey the simple, natural rules which make it so."

He smiled at me as he said, "Man is a mere speck in a troubled world. Man is only comfortable when feeling safe in some form of 'Mother's embrace.' For those in the West, untrained in the art of dying, the last thought, the last cry, is 'Mother!' A man who is unsure of himself while trying to give an appearance of confidence will suck a cigar or cigarette just as a baby will suck a finger. Psychologists agree that the smoking habit is merely a reversion to the traits of early childhood where a baby drew nourishment *and* confidence from his mother. Religion is a comforter. Knowledge of the truth of life—and death—is of even greater comfort. We are like water when on Earth, like steam when we pass over in 'death' and we condense again to water when we are reborn to this world once more."

"Sir!" I exclaimed, "do you think that children should *not* honour their parents?" My Guide looked at me in some surprise; "Good gracious, Lobsang, of course children should pay respect to their parents—so long as the parents merit it. Over-dominant parents should not be permitted to ruin their children, though, and an adult 'child' certainly has first responsibility to his or her wife or husband. Parents should *not* be permitted to tyrannise and dictate to their adult offspring. To allow parents to act thus is to harm the parents as well as oneself; it makes a debt which the parents must pay in some other life." I thought of my parents. My stern and harsh father, a father who had never been a 'father' to me. My mother whose main thought was of the social life. Then I thought of the Lama Mingyar Dondup who was *more* than a mother and father to me, the only person who had shown me kindness and love at all times.

A monk-messenger hastened in and bowed deeply. "Honourable Lord Mingyar," he said respectfully, "I am commanded to convey to you the respects and salutations of the Inmost One and to ask you to be good enough to go to Him. May I lead you to Him, Sir?" My Guide rose to his feet and accompanied the messenger.

I walked out and climbed to the roof of the Potala. Slightly higher, the Medical Lamasery of Chakpori loomed out of the night. By my side a Prayer Flag flapped weakly against its mast. Standing in a nearby window I saw an old monk busily twirling his Prayer Wheel, its 'clack-clack' a loud sound in the silence of the night. The stars stretched overhead in endless procession, and I wondered, did *we* look like that to some other creature, somewhere?

CHAPTER FOUR

The season was that of Logsar, the Tibetan New Year. We chelas—and trappas also—had been busy for some time now, making butter images. Last year we had not bothered and had therefore occasioned some ill feeling; other lamaseries had held to the belief (correctly!) that we of Chakpori had neither time nor interest for such childish pursuits. This year, then, by order of the Inmost One Himself, we had to make butter images and enter the contest. Our effort was a modest one compared to that of some lamaseries. On a wooden framework, some twenty feet high by thirty feet long, we were moulding in coloured butter various scenes from the Sacred Books. Our figures were fully three-dimensional, and we hoped that when seen by the light of the flickering butter lamps there would be an illusion of movement.

The Inmost One Himself, and all the senior lamas, viewed the exhibits every year and much praise was accorded the builders of the winning effort. After the Season of Logsar the butter was melted down and used in the butter lamps throughout the year. As I worked—I had some skill in modelling—I thought of all that I had learned during the past few months. Certain things about religion still puzzled me and I resolved to ask my Guide the Lama Mingyar Dondup about them at the first opportunity, but now *butter sculpture* was the thing! I stooped and scraped up a fresh load of flesh-coloured butter and carefully climbed up the scaffolding so that I could build up the ear to Buddha-like proportions. Off to my right two young chelas were having a butter ball fight, scooping up hand loads of butter, moulding the stuff roughly round, then throwing that messy missile at the "enemy." They were having a great time, unfortunately a monk-proctor appeared round a stone pillar to see what all the noise was about. Without a word he seized both boys, one in his right hand and the other in his left and threw them both into a great vat of warm butter!

I turned and got on with my work. Butter mixed with lamp-black formed very suitable eyebrows. Already there was illusion of life in the figure. "This *is* the World of Illusion, after all," I thought. Down I climbed, and walked across the floor so that I could obtain a better impression of the work. The Master of the Arts smiled upon me; I was perhaps his favourite pupil as I liked modelling and painting and really worked to learn from him. "We are doing well, Lobsang," he said pleasantly, "the Gods look alive." He walked away in order that he could direct alterations to another part of the scene and I thought, "The Gods look alive! *Are* there Gods? Why are we taught about them if there are none? I must ask my Guide."

Thoughtfully I scraped the butter from my hands. Over in the corner the two chelas who had been thrown into the warm butter were trying to get themselves clean by rubbing their bodies with fine brown sand, looking very foolish indeed as they rubbed away. I chuckled and turned to go. A heavy-set chela walked beside me and remarked, "Even the Gods must have laughed at that!" "Even the Gods—Even the Gods—Even the Gods" the refrain echoed through my mind in time with my footsteps. The Gods, *were* there Gods? I walked on down to the Temple and settled myself waiting for the familiar service to commence. "Hear the Voices of our Souls, all you who wander. This is the World of Illusion. Life is but a dream. All that are born must die." The priest's voice droned on, reciting the well-known words, words which now struck at my curiosity: "The third stick of incense is lit to summon a wandering ghost that he may be guided." "Not helped by the Gods," I thought, "but guided by *his fellow men,* why not by the Gods? Why did we pray to our *Overself* and not to a God?" The rest of the service had no attraction, no meaning for me. I was jolted out of my thoughts by an elbow digging violently into my ribs. "Lobsang! *Lobsang!* What is the matter with you, are you *dead?* Get up, the service is over!" I stumbled to my feet and followed the others out of the Temple.

"Sir!" I said to my Guide the Lama Mingyar Dondup some hours later, "Sir! *Is* there a God? Or Gods?" He looked down at me and said, "Let us go and sit on the roof, Lobsang, we can hardly talk here in this crowded place." He turned and led the way along the corridor, out through the Lamas' quarters, up the notched pole and so on to the roof. For a moment we stood looking at the well-loved scene, the towering mountain ranges, the bright water of the Kyi Chu, and the reed-girt Kaling Chu. Beneath us the Norbu Linga, or Jewel Park, showed as a mass of living green. My Guide waved his hand. "Do you think all *this* is chance, Lobsang? *Of course* there is a God!" We moved to the highest part of the roof and sat down.

"You are confused in your thinking, Lobsang," stated my Guide. "There is a God; there are Gods. While upon this Earth we are in no position to appreciate the Form and Nature of God. We live in what may be termed a three-dimensional world. God lives in a world so far removed that the human brain *while on earth,* cannot hold the necessary concept of God and thus men tend to rationalise. 'God' is assumed to be something human, superhuman if you prefer the term, but Man, in his conceit, believes that he is made in the Image of God! Man also believes that there is no life on other worlds. If Man is made in the Image of God and the peoples of other worlds are in a different image—what is to become of our concept that Man *only* is made in God's Image?" The Lama looked keenly at me to make sure that I was following his remarks. Most certainly I was; all this appeared self-evident.

"Every world, every country of every world, has its

61

God, or Guardian Angel. We call the God in charge of the world the Manu. He is a highly evolved Spirit, a human who through incarnation after incarnation has been purged of the dross, leaving only the pure behind. There is a band of Great Beings who at times of need come to this Earth that they may set an example whereby ordinary mortals may be enabled to lift from the mire of worldly desires."

I nodded my head; I knew about this, knew that Buddha, Moses, Christ and many others were of that Order. I knew also of Maitreya, who, it is stated in the Buddhist Scriptures, will come to the world 5,656 *million* years after the passing of Buddha, or Guatama as He should more accurately be named. All this, and more, was part of our standard religious teachings as was the knowledge that *any* good person had an equal chance no matter what name his own religious belief carried. We never believed that only one religious sect "went to Heaven," and all others were tumbled down to Hell for the amusement of sundry sanguinary fiends. But my Guide was ready to continue.

"We have the Manu of the world, the Great Evolved Being who controls the destiny of the world. There are minor Manus who control the destiny of a country. In endless years, the World Manu will move on, and the next best, now well trained, will evolve, will take over the Earth." "Ah!" I exclaimed in some triumph, "then not all Manus are good! The Manu of Russia is allowing Russians to act against our good. The Manu of China permits the Chinese to raid our borders and kill our people." The Lama smiled across at me. "You forget, Lobsang," he replied, "this world is Hell, we come here to learn lessons. We come here to suffer that our *spirit* may evolve. Hardship teaches, pain teaches, kindness and consideration do not. There are wars in order that men may show courage on the battlefields and—like iron ore in the furnace—be tempered and strengthened by the fire of battle. The flesh body does not matter, Lobsang, that is only a temporary puppet. The Soul, the Spirit, the Overself (call it what you will) is all that need be considered. On Earth, in our blindness, we think that the body alone matters. Fear that the body may suffer clouds our outlook and warps our judgment. We have to act for the good of our own Over-selves, while still assisting others. Those who follow blindly the dictates of overbearing parents add a load to the parents as well as to themselves. Those who blindly follow the dictates of some stereotyped religious belief also cramp their evolution."

"Honourable Lama!" I expostulated, "may I add two comments?" "Yes, you may," replied my Guide. "You said that we learn more quickly if conditions are harsh. I would prefer a little more kindness. I could learn that way." He looked thoughtfully at me. "Could you?" he asked. "Would you learn the Sacred Books even if you did not fear the teachers? Would you do your share in the kitchens if you did not fear punishment if you lazed? Would you?" I hung my head, it was right. I worked in the kitchens when ordered to. I studied the Sacred Books because I feared the result of failure. "And your next question?" asked the Lama. "Well, Sir, how does a stereo-typed religion injure one's evolution?" "I will give you two examples," replied my Guide. "The Chinese believed that it did not matter what they did in this life as they could pay for faults and sins when they came again. Thus they adopted a policy of mental slothfulness. Their religion became as an opiate and drugged them into spiritual laziness; they lived only for the next life, and so their arts and crafts fell into disuse. China thus became a third-rate power in which bandit war-lords started a reign of terror and pillage."

I had noticed that the Chinese in Lhasa seemed to be unnecessarily brutal and quite fatalistic. Death to them meant nothing more than passing to another room! I did not fear death in any way, but I wanted to get my task finished in one lifetime instead of slacking, and having to come to this World time after time. The process of being born, being a helpless baby, having to go to school, all

63

that to me was *trouble*. I hoped that this life would be my last on Earth. The Chinese had had wonderful inventions, wonderful works of art, a wonderful culture. Now, through too slavishly adhering to a religious belief, the Chinese people had become decadent, a ready prey to Communism. At one time age and learning had been deeply respected in China, as should be the case, now—no more were the sages given the honour due to them; all that mattered now was violence, personal gain and selfishness.

"Lobsang!" The Voice of my Guide broke in to my thoughts. "We have seen a religion which taught inaction, which taught that one should not in any way influence another in case one added to one's own Karma—the debt which passes on from life to life." He looked out across the City of Lhasa, seeing our peaceful Valley, then turned to me again. "Religions of the West tend to be very militant. People there are not content to believe what *they* want to believe, but they are willing to kill others to make them believe the same." "I don't see how *killing* a person would be good religious practice," I remarked. "No, Lobsang," replied the Lama, "but in the time of the Spanish Inquisition one branch of Christians tortured any other branch in order that they might be 'converted and saved.' People were stretched on the rack and burned at the stake that they might thus be persuaded to change their belief! Even now these people send out missionaries who try by almost any means to obtain converts. It seems that they are so unsure of their belief that they must have others express approval and agreement of their religion—on the lines, presumably, that there is safety in numbers!"

"Sir!" I said, "do you think people should follow a religion?" "Why, certainly, if they so desire," replied the Lama Mingyar Dondup. "If people have not yet reached the stage where they can accept the Overself, and the Manu of the World, then it may be a comfort for them to adhere to some formal system of religion. It is a mental and spiritual discipline, it makes some people feel that they belong within a family group, with a benevolent Father

64

watching over them, and a compassionate Mother ever ready to intercede on their behalf with the Father. Yes, for those in a certain stage of evolution, such religion is good. But the sooner such people realise that they should pray to their Overself the sooner will they evolve. We are sometimes asked why we have Sacred Images in our Temples, or why we have Temples at all. To that we can reply that such Images are reminders that we too can evolve and in time become high Spiritual Beings. As for our Temples, they are places where people of like mind may congregate for the purpose of giving mutual strength in the task of reaching one's Overself. By prayer, even when that prayer be not properly directed, one is able to reach a higher rate of vibration. Meditation and contemplation within a Temple, a Synagogue, or Church is beneficial."

I mused upon that which I had just heard. Below us the Kaling Chu tinkled and ran faster as it squeezed to crowd itself beneath the Bridge of the Lingkor Road. Off to the south I perceived a party of men waiting for the Ferryman of the Kyi Chu. Traders had come earlier in the day, bringing papers and magazines for my Guide. Papers from India, and from strange countries of the world. The Lama Mingyar Dondup had travelled far and often, and kept in close touch with affairs outside Tibet. Papers, magazines. I had a thought at the back of my mind. Something that had bearing on this discussion. Papers? Suddenly I jumped as if stung. Not papers, but a magazine! Something I had seen, now what was it? I knew! It was all clear to me; I had flicked over some pages, not understanding a single word of the foreign languages, but seeking pictures. One such page had stopped beneath my questing thumb. The picture of a winged being hovering in the clouds, hovering above a field of bloody battle. My Guide, to whom I had shown the picture, had read and translated for me the caption.

"Honourable Lama!" I exclaimed excitedly, "earlier today you told me of that Figure—you called it the Angel of Mons—which many men claimed to see above a battlefield. Was that a God?" "No, Lobsang," replied my Guide, "many many men, in the hour of their desperation, longed to see the figure of a Saint, or as they term it, an Angel. Their urgent need and strong emotions inherent in a battlefield gave strength to their thoughts, their desires, and their prayers. Thus, in the manner of which I have shown you, they formed a thought form to their own specifications. As the first ghostly outline of a figure appeared, the prayers and thoughts of the men who caused it were intensified, and so the figure gained in strength and solidity and persisted for an appreciable time. We do the same thing here when we 'raise thought-forms' in the Inner Temple. But come, Lobsang, the day is far advanced and the Ceremonies of Logsar are not yet concluded."

We walked down the corridor, down into the scene of bustle, the busy turmoil which was the everyday life within a lamasery during a Season of Celebration. The Master of the Arts came in search of me, wanting a small, light boy to climb the scaffold and make some alterations to the head of a figure at the top. Trailing in the Master's wake, I followed him at a brisk pace down the slippery path to the Butter Room. I donned an old robe, one liberally coated with coloured butter, and tying a light line around my waist that I might haul up material, I climbed the scaffold. It was as the Master had surmised, part of the head had broken away from the wooden slats. Calling down what I wanted, I dangled my rope and pulled up a pail of butter. For some hours I worked, twisting slivers of thin wood round the struts of the backing, moulding once again the butter to hold the head in place. At long last, the Master of the Arts, watching critically from the ground, indicated that he was satisfied. Slowly, stiffly, I disentangled myself from the scaffolding and slowly descended to the ground. Thankfully I changed my robe and hurried off.

The next day I and many other chelas were down on the Plain of Lhasa, at the foot of the Potala, by the Village of Shö. In theory we were watching the processions, the games, and the races. In actuality we were showing off in front of the humble pilgrims who thronged the mountain paths that they might be in Lhasa at the time of Logsar. From all over the Buddhist world they came, to this, the Mecca of Buddhism. Old men crippled with age, young women carrying small babies, all came in the belief that in completing the Holy Circuit of the City and the Potala, they were atoning for past sins and ensuring a good rebirth to the next life on Earth. Fortune tellers thronged the Lingkor Road, ancient beggars whined for alms, and traders with their goods suspended from their shoulders pushed their way through the throngs in search of customers. Soon I tired of the frenzied scene, tired of the gaping multitude and their endless, inane questions. I slipped away from my companions and slowly wandered up the mountain path to my lamastic home.

Upon the roof, in my favourite spot, all was quiet. The sun provided a gentle warmth. From below me, now out of sight, there arose a confused murmur from the crowds, a murmur which in its indistinctness, soothed me and made me drowse in the noonday heat. A shadowy figure materialised almost at the extreme limit of my vision. Sleepily I shook my head and blinked my eyes. When I again opened them the figure was still there, clearer now and growing more dense. The hairs at the back of my neck rose in sudden fright. "You are not a ghost!" I exclaimed. "Who are you?" The Figure smiled slightly and replied, "No, my son, I am not a ghost. Once I too studied here at the Chakpori, and lazed as you are lazing now upon this roof. Then I desired above all to speed my liberation from Earthly desires. I had myself immured within the walls of that hermitage," he gestured upwards, and I turned to follow the direction of his outstretched arm. "Now," he continued, telepathically, "on this the eleventh Logsar since that date I have attained that which I sought; freedom to roam at will, while leaving my body safe within the hermitage cell. My first journey is to here, that I may once again gaze upon the crowd, that I may once again visit this

67

well-remembered spot. Freedom, boy, I have attained freedom." Before my gaze he vanished like a cloud of incense dispersed by the night wind.

The hermitages! We chelas had heard so much about them, what were they like inside? We often wondered. Why did men incarcerate themselves within those rock chambers, perched precariously upon the mountain's edge? We wondered about that too! I determined that I would ask my beloved Guide. Then I remembered that an old Chinese Monk lived a few yards from where I was. Old Wu Hsi had had an interesting life; for some years he had been a monk attached to the Palace of the Emperors in Peking. Tiring of such life, he had wandered into Tibet in search of enlightenment. Eventually he had reached the Chakpori, and had been accepted. Tiring of that after a few years, he had gone to a hermitage and for seven years had lived the solitary life. Now, though, he was back at Chakpori waiting to die. I turned and hastened to the corridor below. Making my way to a small cell, I called to the old man.

"Come in! Come in!" he called in a high, quavering voice. I entered his cell, and for the first time met Wu Hsi the Chinese monk. He was sitting cross-legged and in spite of his age his back was as straight as a young bamboo. He had high cheekbones, and very very yellow, parchment-like skin. His eyes were jet black and slanted. A few straggly hairs grew from his chin, and from his upper lip depended a dozen or so hairs of his long moustache. His hands were yellow-brown, and mottled with great age, while his veins stood out like the twigs of a tree. As I walked toward him he peered blindly in my direction, sensing rather than seeing. "Hmmm, hmmm," he said, "a boy, a young boy from the way you walk. What do you want, boy?" "Sir!" I replied, "you lived for long in a hermitage. Will you, Holy Sir, have the goodness to tell me of it?" He mumbled and chewed at the ends of his moustache and then said, "Sit, boy, it is long since I talked of the past, although I think of it constantly now."

68

"When I was a boy," he said, "I travelled far and went to India. There I saw the hermits encloistered within their caves, and some of them appeared to have attained to enlightenment." He shook his head; "The ordinary people were very lazy, spending their days beneath the trees. Ah! It was a sad sight!" "Holy Sir!" I interrupted, "I should much prefer to hear of the hermitages of Tibet." "Eh? What's that?" he asked feebly. "Oh yes, the hermitages of Tibet. I returned from India and went to my native Peking. Life there bored me, for I was not learning. I took again my staff and my bowl and made my way, over many months, to the borders of Tibet." I sighed to myself in exasperation. The old man continued, "In course of time, after having stayed at lamasery after lamasery, always in search of enlightenment, I reached Chakpori. The Abbot permitted me to stay here as I was qualified as a physician in China. My speciality was acupuncture. For a few years I was content, then I conceived a great desire to enter a hermitage." By now I was almost dancing with impatience. If the old man took much longer I should be too late—I could not miss evening service! Even as I thought of it, I could hear the first booming of the gongs. Reluctantly I rose to my feet and said, "Respected sir, I have to go now." The old man chuckled. "No, boy," he replied, "you may stay, for are you not here receiving instruction from an Elder Brother? Stay, you are excused from evening service." I seated myself again, knowing that he was correct; although he was still a trappa, and not a lama, yet still he was considered as an Elder because of his age, his travels, and his experience. "Tea boy, tea!" he exclaimed, "we will have tea, for the flesh is frail and the weight of the years press heavily upon me. Tea, for the young and for the old." In response to his summons, a Monk Attendant to the Aged brought us tea and barley. We mixed our tsampa, and settled down, he to talk and I to listen.

"The Lord Abbot gave me permission to leave Chakpori and enter a hermitage. With a monk-attendant I journeyed from this place and ascended in to the mountains. After five days of travel we reached a spot which may be discerned from the roof above us." I nodded, I knew the place, a solitary building set high in the Himalayas. The old man continued. "This place was empty, the former occupant had recently died. The Attendant and I cleaned out the place then I stood and looked out across the Valley of Lhasa for the last time. I looked down at the Potala and at Chakpori, then turned and went into the inner chamber. The Attendant walled up the door, cementing it firmly, and I was alone." "But Sir! What is it *like* inside?" I asked.

Old Wu Hsi rubbed his head. "It is a stone building," he replied slowly. "A building with very thick walls. There is no door once one is inside the inner chamber because the doorway is walled up. In the wall there is a trap, entirely lightproof, through which the hermit received food. A dark tunnel connects the inner chamber with the room wherein lives the Attendant. I was walled in. The darkness was so thick that I could almost feel it. Not a glimmer of light entered, nor could any sound be heard. I sat upon the floor and began my meditation. First I suffered from hallucinations, imagining that I saw streaks and bands of light. Then I felt the darkness strangling me as if I were covered in soft, dry mud. Time ceased to exist. Soon I heard, in my imagination, bells, and gongs, and the sound of men chanting. Later I beat against the constraining walls of my cell, trying in my frenzy to force a way out. I knew not the difference between day or night, for here all was as black and as silent as the grave. After some time I grew calm, my panic subsided."

I sat and visualised the scene, old Wu Hsi—young Wu Hsi then!—in the almost living darkness within the all-pervading silence. "Every two days," said the old man, "the attendant would come and place a little tsampa outside the trap. Come so silently that I could never hear him. The first time, feeling blindly for my food in the darkness, I knocked it off and could not reach it. I called and screamed, but no sound escaped from my cell; I just had to wait for another two days." "Sir!" I asked, "what happens if a hermit is ill, or dies?" "My boy," said old Wu Hsi, "if a hermit is ill—he dies. The attendant places food every two days for fourteen days. After fourteen days, if the food is still untouched, men come and break down the wall and take out the body of the hermit."

Old Wu Hsi had been a hermit for seven years. "What happens in a case like yours, when you have stayed for the time decided upon?" "I stayed for two years and then for seven. When it was almost time for me to come out the smallest of small holes was made in the ceiling so that a very minute shaft of light entered. Every few days the hole was enlarged, permitting more light to enter. At last I could withstand the full light of day. If the hermit is suddenly brought out into the light he is immediately struck blind as his eyes have been so long dilated in the darkness that they can no longer contract. When I came out I was white, bleached white, and my hair was as white as the mountain snows. I had massage and did exercise, for my muscles were almost useless with disuse. Gradually I recovered my strength until at last I was able with my attendant to descend the mountain to reside again at Chakpori."

I pondered his words, thinking of the endless years of darkness, of utter silence, thrown upon his own resources, and I wondered, "What did you learn from it, Sir?" I asked at last, "was it *worth* it?" "Yes, boy, yes, it was worth it!" said the old monk. "I learned the nature of life, I learned the purpose of the brain. I became free of the body and could send my spirit soaring afar just as you do now in the astral." "But how do you know that you did not imagine it? How do you know you were sane? *Why* could you not travel in the astral as I do?" Wu Hsi laughed until the tears rolled down his furrowed cheeks. "Questions—questions—questions, boy, just as I used to ask them!" he replied.

"First I was overcome by panic. I cursed the day I became a monk, cursed the day I entered the cell. Gradually

71

I was able to follow the breathing patterns and to meditate. At the start I had hallucinations, vain imaginings. Then one day I slipped free of my body and the darkness was dark no more to me. I saw my body sitting in the attitude of meditation. I saw my sightless, staring wide-open eyes. I saw the pallor of my skin and the thinness of my body. Rising, I passed through the roof of the cell and saw below me the Valley of Lhasa. I saw certain alterations, saw people with whom I was acquainted and, passing into the Temple, I was able to converse with a telepathic lama who confirmed my release for me. I wandered far and wide and beyond the borders of this country. Every two days I returned and entered my body, re-animating it that I might eat and nourish it." "But why could you not do astral travelling without all that preparation?" I asked again.

"Some of us are very ordinary mortals. Few of us have the special ability given to you by virtue of the task you have to undertake. You too have travelled far by the astral way. Others, such as I, have to endure solitude and hardship before their spirit can break free from the flesh. You, boy, are one of the fortunate ones, one of the *very* fortunate ones!" The old man sighed, and said, "Go! I must rest, I have talked long. Come and see me again, you will be a welcome visitor in spite of your questions." He turned away, and with a muttered word of thanks I rose to my feet, bowed, and slipped quietly from the room. I was so busy thinking that I walked straight into the opposite wall and almost knocked my spirit out of my body. Rubbing my aching head, I walked sedately along the corridor until I reached my own cell.

The midnight service was almost over. Monks were fidgeting slightly, ready to hurry off for a few more hours of sleep before returning. The old Reader up on the podium carefully inserted a marker between the pages of the Book and turned in readiness to step down. Sharp eyed proctors, ever alert for disturbances, or for inattentive small boys, relaxed their gazes. The service was almost over. Small chelas swung the censers for the last pass, and there was the barely suppressed hum of a large gathering preparing to move. Suddenly there was an ear-splitting screech, and a wild figure bounded over the heads of the sitting monks and tried to seize a young trappa holding two sticks of incense. We jerked upright with shock. Before us the wild figure whirled and spun, foam flying from writhing lips, hideous screams pouring from tortured throat. For a moment of time the world seemed to stand still; police-monks frozen into immobility with surprise, officiating priests standing with arms upraised. Then violently, the proctors swung into action. Converging on the mad figure, they quickly subdued him, winding his robe about his head to silence the evil oaths which streamed in a torrent from his mouth. Efficiently, speedily, he was lifted and removed from the Temple. The service ended. We rose to our feet and hastened out, anxious to get beyond the Temple bounds so that we could discuss that which we had just seen.

"That's Kenji Tekeuchi," said a young trappa near me. "He is a Japanese monk who has been visiting everywhere." "Been around the world, so they say," added another. "Searching for Truth, and hoping to get it handed to him instead of working for it," remarked a third. I wandered off, somewhat troubled in mind. *Why* should 'Searching for Truth' make a man mad? The room was cold, and I shivered slightly as I wrapped my robe around me and lay down to sleep. It seemed that no time at all had elapsed before the gongs were booming again for the next service. As I looked through the window I saw the first rays of the sun come over the mountains, rays of light like giant fingers probing the sky, reaching for the stars. I sighed, and hurried down the corridor, anxious not to be the last one to enter the Temple and thus merit the wrath of the proctors.

"You are looking thoughtful, Lobsang," said my Guide the Lama Mingyar Dondup when I saw him later in the day, after the noon service. He motioned for me to sit.

"You saw the Japanese monk, Kenji Tekeuchi, when he entered the Temple. I want to tell you about him, for later you will meet him." I settled myself more comfortably, this was not going to be a quick session—I was 'caught' for the rest of the day! The Lama smiled as he saw my expression. "Perhaps we should have Indian tea . . . and Indian sweetcakes . . . to sugar the pill, Lobsang, eh?" I brightened up a bit, and he chuckled and said, "The attendant is bringing it now, I expected you!" "Yes," I thought, as the monk-servant entered, "where else would I have such a Teacher?" The cakes from India were my special favourites, and even the Lama's eyes sometimes widened with astonishment at the number I could 'put away'!

"Kenji Tekeuchi," said my Guide, "is—was—a very versatile man. A well travelled one. Throughout his life (he is now over seventy) he has wandered the world in search of what he calls 'Truth'. Truth is within him, yet he knows it not. Instead he has wandered, and wandered again. Always he has been studying religious beliefs, always he has been reading the books of many lands in pursuit of this search, this obsession. Now, at long last, he has been sent to us. He has read so much of a conflicting nature that his aura is contaminated. He has read so much and understood so little that most of the time he is insane. He is a human sponge, mopping up all knowledge and digesting very little." "Then, Sir!" I exclaimed, "you are opposed to book-study?" "Not at all, Lobsang," replied the Lama, "I am opposed, as are all thinking men, to those who obtain the brochures, the pamphlets, and the books written about strange cults, about so-called occultism. These people *poison* their soul, they make further progress impossible for them until they have shed all the false knowledge and become as a little child."

"Honourable Lama," I asked, "*how* does one become insane; *how* does wrong reading sometimes lead to confusion?" "That is quite a long story," replied the Lama Mingyar Dondup. "First we have to deal with some fundamentals. Possess yourself in patience and listen! Upon Earth we are as puppets, puppets made of vibrating molecules surrounded by an electric charge. Our Overself vibrates at a very much higher rate, and has a very much higher electric charge. There is a definite relationship between our rate of vibration and that of our Overself. One can liken the process of communication between each one of us on this Earth and our Overself elsewhere to a new process on this world, the process whereby radio waves are sent across continents and seas, thus enabling a person in one country to communicate with a person in a far distant land. Our brains are similar to radio receivers in that they receive the 'high frequency' messages, orders and instructions, from the Overself and turn them into low frequency impulses which control our actions. The brain is the electro-mechanical-chemical device which makes us useful on Earth. Chemical reactions cause our brain to function in a faulty manner by perhaps blocking part of a message, for rarely, on Earth, do we receive the *exact* message 'broadcast' by the Overself. The Mind is capable of limited action without reference to the Overself. The Mind is able to accept certain responsibilities, form certain opinions, and attempts to bridge the gap between the 'ideal' conditions of the Overself and the difficult ones of Earth."

"But do Western people accept the theory of electricity in the brain?" I asked. "Yes," replied my Guide, "in certain hospitals the brain waves of patients are charted, and it has been found that certain mental disorders have a characteristic brain-wave pattern. Thus, from the brain waves it can be stated that a person does or does not suffer from some mental disease or illness. Often an illness of the body will send certain chemicals to the brain, contaminate its wave-form, and thus give symptoms of insanity." "Is the Japanese very mad?" I asked. "Come! We will see him now, he has one of his lucid spells." The Lama Mingyar Dondup rose to his feet and hurried from the room. I jumped to my feet and sped after him. He led the way on down the corridor, down to another level, and to a distant wing where lodged those undergoing medical treatment. In a little alcove, overlooking the Khati Linga, the Japanese monk sat looking moodily outwards. At the approach of the Lama Mingyar Dondup he rose to his feet, clasped his hands and bowed low. "Be seated," said my Guide. "I have brought a young man to you that he may listen to your words. He is under special instruction by order of the Inmost One." The Lama bowed, turned and left the alcove. For some moments the Japanese stared at me, then motioned for me to sit. I sat—at a discreet distance as I did not know when he would become violent!

"Do not cram your head with all the occult stuff you can read, boy!" said the Japanese monk. "It is indigestible matter which will impede your spiritual progress. I studied all the Religions. I studied all the metaphysical cults which I could find. It poisoned me, clouded my outlook, led me to believe that I was a Specially Chosen One. Now my brain is impaired and at times I lose control of myself— escape from the direction of my Overself." "But Sir!" I exclaimed, "how may one learn if one may not read? What possible harm can come of the printed word?" "Boy!" said the Japanese monk, "certainly one may read, but choose with care what you read and make sure that you quite understand that which you are reading. There is no danger in the printed word, but there *is* danger in the thoughts which those words may cause. One should not eat everything, mixing the compatible with the incompatible; nor should one read things which contradict or oppose others, nor should one read things which promise occult powers. It is easily possible to make a Thought-form which one cannot control, as I did, and the Form injures one." "Have you been to all the countries of the world?" I asked. The Japanese looked at me, and a slight twinkle appeared in his eyes.

"I was born in a small Japanese village," he said, "and when I was old enough I entered Holy Service. For years I studied religions and occult practices. Then my Superior told me to leave and to travel in countries far beyond the

76

oceans. For fifty years I have travelled from country to country, from continent to continent, always studying. By my thoughts I have created Powers which I could not control. Powers that live in the astral plane and which at times affect my Silver Cord. Later maybe I shall be permitted to tell you more. For the present, I am still weak from the last attack and thus must rest. With the permission of your Guide you may visit me at a later date." I made my bows and left him alone in the alcove. A medical monk, seeing me leave, hastened in to him. Curiously I peeped about me, peeped at the old monks lying there in this part of the Chakpori. Then, in response to an urgent telepathic call, I hastened away to my Guide, the Lama Mingyar Dondup.

CHAPTER FIVE

I hurried along the corridors, rushing round corners to the peril of those who got in my way. An old monk grabbed me in passing, shook me, and said, "It is not good to have this unseemly haste, boy, it is not the way of the true Buddhist!" Then he peered into my face, recognised me as the ward of the Lama Mingyar Dondup. With a muttered sound that appeared to be *"ulp!"* he dropped me like a hot coal and *hastened* on his way. I sedately followed my own course. At the entrance to my Guide's room I stopped with such a jerk that I almost fell over; with him were two very senior abbots. My conscience was giving me a very bad time; *what* had I done now? Worse, which of my many 'sins' had been discovered? Senior abbots did not wait for small boys unless it was bad news for the small boys. My legs felt distinctly rubbery and I ransacked my memory to see if I had done anything that could cause my expulsion from Chakpori. One of the abbots looked at me and smiled with the warmth of an old iceberg. The other looked toward me with a face that seemed carved from a piece of the Himalayas. My Guide laughed, "You certainly have a guilty conscience, Lobsang. Ah! These Reverend Brother Abbots are also telepathic lamas," he added with a chuckle.

The grimmer of the two abbots looked hard at me, and in a voice reminiscent of falling rocks said, "Tuesday Lobsang Rampa, The Inmost One has caused investigation to be made whereby it has been determined that you be Recognised as the present Incarnation of . . ." My head was awhirl, I could hardly follow what he was saying, and barely caught his concluding remarks, ". . . and the style, rank, and title of Lord Abbot be conferred upon you by virtue of this at a ceremony the time and place of which shall be determined at a later occasion." The two abbots bowed solemnly to the Lama Mingyar Dondup, and then bowed as solemnly to me. Picking up a book, they filed out and gradually the sound of their footfalls became no more. I stood as one dazed, gazing down the corridor after them. A hearty laugh, and the clasp of a hand on my shoulder brought me back to the present. "Now you know what all the running about was for. The tests have merely confirmed what we knew all the time. It calls for a special celebration between you and me, then I have some interesting news for you." He led me into another room, and there was a spread a real Indian meal. Without any need to be encouraged, I set to!

Later, when I could eat no more, when even the sight of the remaining food made me feel queasy, my Guide rose and led the way back into the other room. "The Inmost One has given me permission to tell you about the Cave of the Ancients," he said, immediately adding, "rather, the Inmost One has suggested that I tell you about it." He gave me a sideways glance, then almost in a whisper, remarked, "We are sending an expedition there within a few days." I felt the excitement surge through me and had the impossible impression that perhaps I was going "home" to a place I had known before. My Guide was watching me very closely indeed. As I looked up, under the intensity of his gaze, he nodded his head. "Like you, Lobsang, I had special training, special opportunities. My own Teacher was a man who long ago passed from this life, whose empty Shell is even now in the Hall of Golden Images. With him I travelled extensively throughout the world. You, Lobsang, will have to travel alone. Now sit still and I will tell you of the finding of the Cave of the Ancients." I wet my lips, this was what I had wanted to hear for some time. In a lamasery, as in every community, rumours were often spread in confidential corners. Some rumours were self-evident as *rumours* and nothing more. This, though, was different, somehow I believed what I had heard.

"I was a very young lama, Lobsang," commenced my Guide. "With my Teacher and three young lamas we were exploring some of the remoter mountain ranges. Some weeks before there had been an extraordinary loud bang, followed by a heavy rock-fall. We were out to investigate matters. For days we had prowled round the base of a mighty rock pinnacle. Early on the morning of the fifth day my Teacher awakened, yet was not awake; he appeared to be in a daze. We spoke to him and received no answer. I was overcome by worry, thinking that he was ill, wondering how we should get him down the endless miles to safety. Sluggishly, as if in the grip of some strange power, he struggled to his feet, fell over, and at last stood upright. Stumbling, jerking, and moving like a man in a trance, he moved ahead. We followed almost in fear and trembling. Up the steep rock face we climbed, with showers of small stones raining down upon us. At last we reached the sharp edge of the range top and stood peering over. I experienced a feeling of deep disappointment; before us was a small valley now almost filled with huge boulders. Here, evidently was where the rock fall had originated. Some rock-fault had developed, or some Earth tremor had occurred which had dislodged part of the mountainside. Great gashes of newly exposed rock glared at us in the bright sunlight. Moss and lichen drooped disconsolately now deprived of any support. I turned away in disgust. There was nothing here to engage my attention, nothing but a rather large rock-fall. I turned to start the descent, but was immediately halted by a whispered 'Mingyar!' One of my companions was pointing. My Teacher, still under some strange compulsion, was edging down the mountainside." I sat enthralled, my Guide stopped talking for a moment and took a sip of water, then continued.

"We watched him with some desperation. Slowly he climbed down the side, toward the rock-strewn floor of the little valley. We reluctantly followed, expecting every moment to slip on that dangerous range. At the bottom, my Teacher did not hesitate, but picked a careful way across the immense boulders, until at last he reached the other side of the stone valley. To our horror he commenced to climb upwards, using hand and foot holds which were invisible to us a few yards behind him. We followed reluctantly. There was no other course open to us, we could not return and say that our senior had climbed from us, that we were afraid to follow him—dangerous though the climb was. I climbed first, picking a very careful way. It was hard rock, the air was thin. Soon the breath was rasping in my throat and my lungs were filled with a harsh, dry ache. Upon a narrow ledge perhaps five hundred feet from the valley, I lay stretched out, gasping for breath. As I glanced up, preparatory to resuming the climb, I saw the yellow robe of my Teacher disappear over a ledge high above. Grimly I clung to the mountain face, edging ever upwards. My companions, as reluctant as I, followed behind. By now we were clear of the shelter afforded by the small valley, and the keen wind was whipping our robes about us. Small stones pelted down and we were hard put to keep going." My Guide paused a moment to take another sip of water and to look to see that I was listening. I was!

"At last," he continued, "I felt a ledge level with my questing fingers. Taking a firm grip, and calling to the others that we had reached a place where we could rest, I pulled myself up. There was a ledge, sloping slightly down towards the back and so quite invisible from the other side of the mountain range. At first glance the ledge appeared to be about ten feet wide. I did not stop to see further, but knelt so that I could help the others up, one by one. Soon we stood together, shivering in the wind after our exertion. Quite obviously the rock fall had uncovered this ledge, and—as I peered more closely, there was a narrow crevice in the mountain wall. Was there? From where we stood it might have been a shadow, or the stain of dark lichen. As one, we moved forward. It *was* a crevice, one that was

81

about two feet six inches wide by about five feet high. Of my Teacher there was no sign." I could visualise the scene well. But this was not the time for introspection. I did not want to miss a word!

"I stepped back to see if my Teacher had climbed higher," my Guide went on, "but there was no sign of him. Fearfully I peered into the crevice. It was as dark as the grave. Inch by inch, painfully bent, I moved inside. About fifteen feet in I turned a very sharp corner, another, and then another. Had I not been paralysed with fright I would have screamed with surprise; here was light, a soft silvery light, brighter than the brightest moonlight. Light that I had never seen before. The cave in which I now found myself was spacious, with a roof invisible in the darkness above. One of my companions pushed me out of the way and was in turn pushed by another. Soon the four of us stood silent and frightened gazing at the fantastic sight before us. A sight which would have made any one of us alone think that he had taken leave of his senses. The cave was more like an immense hall, it stretched away in the distance as if the mountain itself was hollow. The light was everywhere, beating down upon us from a number of globes which appeared to be suspended from the darkness of the roof. Strange machines crammed the place, machines such as we could not have imagined. Even from the high roof depended apparatus and mechanisms. Some, I saw with great amazement, were covered by what appeared to be the clearest of glass." My eyes must have been round with amazement, for the Lama smiled at me before resuming his story.

"By now we had quite forgotten my Teacher, when he suddenly appeared we jumped straight off the ground in fright! He chuckled at our staring eyes and stricken faces. Now, we saw, he was no longer in the grip of that strange, overpowering compulsion. Together we wandered round looking at the strange machines. To us they had no meaning, they were just collections of metal and fabric in strange, exotic form. My Teacher moved toward a rather large black panel apparently built into one of the walls of the cave. As he was about to feel its surface it swung open. By now we were almost at the point of believing that the whole place was bewitched, or that we had fallen prey to some hallucinating force. My Teacher jumped back in some alarm. The black panel swung shut. Greatly daring one of my companions stretched out his hand and the panel swung open again. A force which we could not resist propelled us forward. Uselessly fighting against every step, we were—somehow—made to enter through the panel doorway. Inside it was dark, as dark as the darkness of a hermit's cell. Still under the irresistible compulsion, we moved in many feet and then sat on the floor. For minutes we sat shivering with fright. As nothing happened we regained some calmness, and then we heard a series of clicks, as if metal were tapping and scraping on metal." Involuntarily I shivered. I had the thought that I probably would have died of fright! My Guide continued.

"Slowly, almost imperceptibly, a misty glow formed in the darkness before us. At first it was just a suspicion of blue-pink light, almost as if a ghost were materialising before our gaze. The mist-light spread, becoming brighter so that we could see the outlines of incredible machines filling this large hall, all except the centre of the floor upon which we sat. The light drew in upon itself, swirling, fading, and becoming brighter and then it formed and remained in spherical shape. I had the strange and unexplainable impression of age-old machinery creaking slowly into motion after eons of time. The five of us huddled together on the floor, literally spellbound. There came a probing inside my brain, as if demented telepathic lamas were playing, then the impression changed and became as clear as speech." My Guide cleared his throat, and reached again for a drink, staying his hand in mid-air. "Let us have tea, Lobsang," he said as he rang his silver bell. The monk-attendant obviously knew what was wanted, for he came in with tea—and cakes!

"Within the sphere of light we saw pictures," said the

83

Lama Mingyar Dondup, "hazy at first, they soon cleared and ceased to be pictures. Instead we actually *saw* the events." I could contain myself no longer: "But Honourable Lama, *what* did you see?" I asked in a fever of impatience. The Lama reached forward and poured himself more tea. It occurred to me then that I had never seen him eat those Indian sweet cakes. Tea, yes, he drank plenty of tea, but I had never known him take anything but the most sparing and the plainest of food. The gongs went for temple service, but the Lama did not stir. When the last of the monks had hurried by he sighed deeply, and said, "Now I will continue."

He resumed. "This is what we saw and heard, and you shall see and hear in the not too distant future. Thousands and thousands of years ago there was a high civilization upon this world. Men could fly through the air in machines which defied gravity; men were able to make machines which would impress thoughts upon the minds of others— thoughts which would appear as pictures. They had nuclear fission, and at last they detonated a bomb which all but wrecked the world, causing continents to sink below the oceans and others to rise. The world was decimated, and so, throughout the religions of this Earth, we now have the story of the Flood." I was unimpressed by this latter part. "Sir!" I exclaimed, "we can see pictures like that in the Akashic Record. Why struggle up dangerous mountains just to see what we can more easily experience here?" "Lobsang," said my Guide gravely, "we can see all in the astral and in the Akashic Record, for the latter contains the knowledge of all that has happened. We can *see* but we cannot *touch*. In astral travel we can go places and return, but we cannot touch anything of the world. We cannot," he smiled slightly, "take even a spare robe nor bring back a flower. So with the Akashic Record, we can see all, but we cannot examine in close detail those strange machines stored in those mountain halls. We are going to the mountains, and we are going to examine the machines."

"How strange," I said, "that these machines should of all the world be only in our country!" "Oh! But you are wrong!" explained my Guide. "There is a similar chamber at a certain place in the country of Egypt. There is another chamber with identical machines located in a place called South America. I have seen them, I know where they are. These secret chambers were concealed by the peoples of old so that their artifacts would be found by a later generation when the time was ready. This sudden rock fall accidentally bared the entrance to the chamber in Tibet, and once inside we gained the knowledge of the other chambers. But the day is far advanced. Soon seven of us—and that includes you—will set out and journey once again to the Cave of the Ancients."

For days I was in a fever of excitement. I had to keep my knowledge to myself. Others were to know that we were going to the mountains on an herb-gathering expedition. Even in such a secluded place as Lhasa there were always those on the constant lookout for financial gain; the representatives of other countries such as China, Russia, and England, some missionaries, and the traders who came from India, they were all ready to listen to where we kept our gold and our jewels, always ready to exploit anything that promised a profit for them. So—we kept the true nature of our expedition very secret indeed.

Some two weeks after that talk with the Lama Mingyar Dondup, we were ready to depart, ready for the long, long climb up the mountains, through little known ravines and craggy paths. The Communists are now in Tibet, so the location of the Cave of the Ancients is deliberately being concealed, for the Cave is a very real place indeed, and possession of the artifacts there would permit the Communists to conquer the world. All this, all that I write is true, except the exact way to that Cave. In a secret place the precise area, complete with references and sketches, has been noted on paper so that—when the time comes—forces of *freedom* can find the place.

Slowly we descended the path from Chakpori Lamasery

and made our way along to the Kashya Linga, passing that Park as we followed the road down to the ferry where the boatman was waiting for us with his inflated yak-hide boat drawn to the side. There were seven of us, including me, and the crossing of the River—the Kyi Chu—took some time. Eventually we were together again on the far bank. Shouldering our loads, food, rope, a spare robe each, and a few metal tools, we set out towards the south-west. We walked until the setting sun and lengthening shadows made it difficult for us to pick our way across the stony path. Then, in the gathering darkness, we had a modest meal of tsampa before settling down to sleep in the lee side of great boulders. I fell asleep almost as soon as my head rested upon my spare robe. Many Tibetan monks of lama grade slept sitting up, as the regulations prescribe. I, and many more slept lying down, but we had to follow the rule that we could sleep only if lying on the right side. My last sight before dropping off to sleep, was that of the Lama Mingyar Dondup sitting like a carved statue against the dark night sky.

At the first light of the dawning day we awakened and had a very frugal meal, then taking up our loads, we marched on. For the whole day we walked, and for the day after. Passing the foothills, we came to the really mountainous ranges. Soon we were reduced to roping ourselves together and sending the lightest man—me!—across dangerous crevices first so that the ropes could be secured to rock pinnacles and thus afford safe passage to the heavier men. So we forged on, climbing up into the mountains. At last, as we stood at the foot of a mighty rock-face, almost devoid of hand and foot holds, my Guide said, "Over this slab, down the other side, across the little valley which we shall find, and we are then at the foot of the Cave." We prowled round the base of the slab, looking for a hand hold. Apparently other rock falls throughout the years had obliterated small ledges and clefts. After wasting almost a day we found a "chimney" of rock up which we climbed using hands and feet and wedging our backs against the other side of the "chimney." Gasping and puffing in the rarefied air, we climbed to the top and looked over. At last before us was the valley. Staring intently at the far wall we could discern no cave, no fissure in the smooth rock surface. The valley below us was littered with great boulders and—far worse—a rushing mountain stream poured along the centre.

Gingerly we climbed down to the valley and made our way to the banks of that fast-running stream until we came to a part where great boulders afforded a precarious passage for those with the ability to leap from rock to rock. I, being the smallest, had not the length of leg for the jumps, and so was ignominiously hauled through the icy torrent at the end of a rope. Another unfortunate, a small somewhat rotund lama, jumped short—and he too was hauled out at the end of a rope. On the far bank we wrung out our soaked robes, and put them on again. Spray made all of us wet to the skin. Picking our way cautiously over the boulders, we crossed the valley and approached the final barrier, the rock slab. My Guide, the Lama Mingyar Dondup, pointed to a fresh rock scar. "Look!" he said, "a further rock fall has knocked off the first ledge by which we climbed." We stood well back, trying to get a view of the ascent before us. The first ledge was about twelve feet above the ground, and there was no other way. The tallest and sturdiest lama stood with his arms outstretched, bracing himself against the rock face, then the lightest of the lamas climbed on to his shoulders and similarly braced himself. At last I was lifted up so that I could climb on to the shoulders of the top man. With a rope around my waist, I eased myself on to the ledge.

Below me the monks called directions, while slowly, almost dying with fright, I climbed higher until I could loop the end of the rope around a projecting pinnacle of rock. I crouched to the side of the ledge as one after the other, the six lamas climbed the rope, passed me, and continued upwards. The last one untied the rope, coiled it around his waist, and followed the others. Soon the end of the rope dangled before me, and a shout warned me to tie a loop about myself so that I could be hauled up. My height was not sufficient to reach all the ledges unaided. I rested again at a much higher stage, and the rope was carried upwards. At last I was hauled to the topmost ledge where the others of the party awaited me. Being kind and considerate men, they had waited for me so that we could all enter the Cave together, and I confess that my heart warmed at their thoughtfulness. "Now we have hauled up the Mascot we can continue!" growled one. "Yes," I replied, "but the smallest one had to move first or *you* would not be here!" They laughed, and turned to the well-concealed crevice.

I looked in considerable astonishment. At first I could not see the entrance, all I saw was a dark shadow looking much like a dried-up watercourse, or the stain of minute lichen. Then, as we crossed the ledge, I saw that there was indeed a crack in the rock face. A big lama grabbed me by the shoulders and pushed me into the rock fissure saying, good-naturedly, "You go first, and then you can chase out any rock devils and so protect us!" So I, the smallest and least important of the party, was the first to enter the Cave of the Ancients. I edged inside, and crept round the rock corners. Behind me I heard the shuffle and scrape as the bulkier men felt their way in. Suddenly the light burst upon me, for the moment almost paralysing me with fright. I stood motionless by the rocky wall, gazing at the fantastic scene within. The Cave appeared to be about twice as large as the interior of the Great Cathedral of Lhasa. Unlike that Cathedral, which always was enshrouded in the dusk which butter lamps tried vainly to dispel, here was brightness more intense than that of the full moon on a cloudless night. No, it was much brighter than that; the quality of the light must have given me the impression of moonlight. I gazed upwards at the globes which provided the illumination. The lamas crowded in beside me, and, like me, they gazed at the source of light first. My Guide said, "The old records indicate that the illumination here

88

was originally much brighter, these lamps are burning low with the passage of hundreds of centuries."

For long moments we stood still, silent, as though afraid of waking those who slept throughout the endless years. Then, moved by a common impulse, we walked across the solid stone floor to the first machine standing dormant before us. We crowded around it, half afraid to touch it yet very curious as to what it could be. It was dulled with age, yet it appeared ready for instant use—if one knew what it was for and how to operate it. Other devices engaged our attention, also without result. These machines were far, far too advanced for us. I wandered off to where a small square platform about three feet wide, with guard rails, rested on the ground. What appeared to be a long, folded metal tube extended from a nearby machine, and the platform was attached to the other end of the tube. Idly I stepped on to the railed square, wondering what it could be. The next instant I almost died of shock; the platform gave a little tremor and rose high into the air. I was so frightened that I clung in desperation to the rails.

Below me the six lamas gazed upwards in consternation. The tube had unfolded and was swinging the platform straight to one of the spheres of light. In desperation I looked over the side. Already I was some thirty feet in the air, and rising. My fear was that the source of light would burn me to a crisp, like a moth in the flame of a butter lamp. There was a *"click"* and the platform stopped. Inches from my face the light glowed. Timidly I stretched out my hand—and the whole sphere was as cold as ice. By now I had regained my composure somewhat, and I gazed about me. Then a chilling thought struck me; *how was I going to get down?* I jumped from side to side, trying to work out a way of escape, but there appeared to be none. I tried to reach the long tube, hoping to climb down, but it was too far away. Just when I was becoming desperate, there was another tremor, and the platform started to descend. Hardly waiting for it to touch ground I leaped out! I was taking no risks that the thing would go up again.

Against a far wall crouched a great statue, one that sent a shiver up my spine. It was of a crouching cat body, but with the head and shoulders of a woman. The eyes appeared to be alive; the face had a half-mocking, half-quizzical expression which rather frightened me. One of the lamas was on his knees on the floor, gazing intently at some strange marks. "Look!" he called, "this picture-writing shows men and cats talking, it shows what is obviously the soul leaving a body and wandering in the under-world." He was consumed with scientific zeal, poring over the pictures on the floor—"hieroglyphs" he called them—and expecting everyone else to be similarly enthused. This Lama was a highly trained man, one who learned ancient languages without any difficulties at all. The others were poking around the strange machines, trying to decide what they were for. A sudden shout made us wheel round in some alarm. The tall thin Lama was at the far wall and he seemed to have his face stuck in a dull metal box. He stood there with his head bent and the whole of his face concealed. Two men rushed to him and dragged him away from the danger. He uttered a roar of wrath and dashed back!

"Strange!" I thought, "even the sedate, learned lamas are going crazy in this place!" Then the tall, thin one moved aside and another took his place. So far as I could gather, they were seeing moving machines in that box. At last my Guide took pity on me and lifted me up to what apparently were "eye pieces." As I was lifted up and put my hands on a handle as instructed, I saw inside the box, men, and the machines which were in this Hall. The men were operating the machines. I saw that the platform upon which I had ascended to the light-sphere could be controlled and was a type of moveable "ladder" or rather a device which would dispense with ladders. Most of the machines here, I observed, were actual working models such as, in later years, I was to see in Science Museums throughout the world.

We moved to the panel which the Lama Mingyar Dondup had told me about previously, and at our approach it opened with a grating creak, so loud in the silence of the place that I think we all jumped with alarm. Inside was the darkness, profound, almost as if we had clouds of blackness swirling about us. Our feet were guided by shallow channels in the floor. We shuffled along, and when the channels ended we sat. As we did so, there came a series of clicks, like metal scraping against metal, and almost imperceptibly light stole across the darkness and pushed it aside. We looked about us and saw more machines, strange machines. There were statues here, and pictures carved in metal. Before we had time to more than glance, the light drew in upon itself and formed a glowing globe in the centre of the Hall. Colours flickered aimlessly, and bands of light without apparent meaning swirled round the globe. Pictures formed, at first blurred and indistinct, then growing vivid and real and with three-dimensional effect. We watched intently ...

This was the world of Long Long Ago. When the world was very young. Mountains stood where now there are seas, and the pleasant seaside resorts are now mountain tops. The weather was warmer and strange creatures roamed afield. This was a world of scientific progress. Strange machines rolled along, flew inches from the surface of the Earth, or flew miles up in the air. Great temples reared their pinnacles skywards, as if in challenge to the clouds. Animals and Man talked telepathically together. But all was not bliss; politicians fought against politicians. The world was a divided camp in which each side coveted the lands of the other. Suspicion and fear were the clouds under which the ordinary man lived. Priests of *both* sides proclaimed that they alone were the favoured of the gods. In the pictures before us we saw ranting priests—as now—purveying their own brand of salvation. At a price! Priests of each sect taught that it was a "holy duty" to kill the enemy. Almost in the same breath they preached that Mankind throughout the world were brothers. The illogicality of brother killing brother did not occur to them.

We saw great wars fought, with most of the casualties being civilians. The armed forces, behind their armour, were mostly safe. The aged, the women and children, those who did not *fight*, were the ones to suffer. We saw glimpses of scientists working in laboratories, working to produce even deadlier weapons, working to produce bigger and better bugs to drop on the enemy. One sequence of pictures showed a group of thoughtful men planning what they termed a "Time Capsule" (what *we* called "The Cave of the Ancients"), wherein they could store for later generations working models of their machines and a complete, pictorial record of their culture and lack of it. Immense machines excavated the living rock. Hordes of men installed the models and the machines. We saw the cold-light spheres hoisted in place, inert radio-active substances giving off light for millions of years. Inert in that it could not harm humans, active in that the light would continue almost until the end of Time itself.

We found that we could understand the language, then the explanation was shown, that we were obtaining the "speech" telepathically. Chambers such as this, or "Time Capsules," were concealed beneath the sands of Egypt, beneath a pyramid in South America, and at a certain spot in Siberia. Each place was marked by the symbol of the times; the Sphinx. We saw the great statues of the Sphinx, which did *not* originate in Egypt, and we received an explanation of its form. Man and animals talked and worked together in those far-off days. The cat was the most perfect animal for power and intelligence. Man himself is an animal, so the Ancients made a figure of a large cat body to indicate power and endurance, and upon the body they put the breasts and head of a woman. The head was to indicate human intelligence and reason, while the breasts indicated that Man and Animal could draw spiritual and mental nourishment each for the other. That Symbol was then as common as are Statues of Buddha, or the Star of David, or the Crucifix at the present day.

We saw oceans with great floating cities which moved from land to land. In the sky floated equally large craft which moved without sound. Which could hover, and almost instantly flash into stupendous speed. On the surface vehicles moved some inches above the ground itself, supported in the air by some method which we could not determine. Bridges stretched across the cities carrying on slender cables what appeared to be roadways. As we watched we saw a vivid flash in the sky, and one of the largest bridges collapsed into a tangle of girders and cables. Another flash, and most of the city itself vanished into incandescent gas. Above the ruins towered a strangely evil-looking red cloud, roughly in the shape of a mushroom miles high.

Our pictures faded, and we saw again the group of men who had planned the "Time Capsules." They had decided that *now* was the time to seal them. We saw the ceremonies, we saw the "stored memories" being fitted into the machine. We heard the speech of farewell which told us—"The People of the Future, if there be any!"—that Mankind was about to destroy itself, or such seemed probable, "and within these vaults are stored such records of our achievements and follies as may benefit those of a future race who have the intelligence to discover it, and having discovered it, be able to understand it." The telepathic voice faded out, the picture screen turned black. We sat in silence, stupefied by what we had seen. Later, as we sat, the light grew again and we saw that it was actually coming from the walls of that room.

We rose and looked about us. This Hall was also littered with machines and there were many models of cities and bridges, all formed of some kind of stone or of some type of metal the nature of which we were unable to determine. Certain of the exhibits were protected by some quite transparent material which baffled us. It was not glass; we just did not know *what* the stuff was, all we knew was that it effectively prevented us from touching some of the models. Suddenly we all jumped; a baleful red eye was watching us, winking at us. I was prepared to run for it when my Guide the Lama Mingyar Dondup strode over to the machine with the red eye. He looked down at it and touched the handles. The red eye vanished. Instead on a small screen we saw a picture of another room leading from the Main Hall. Into our brains came a message, "As you leave, go to the room (???) where you will find materials with which to seal any opening through which you entered. If you have not reached the stage of evolution where you can work our machines, seal this place and leave it intact for those who will come later."

Silently we filed out into the third room, the door of which opened at our approach. It contained many carefully sealed canisters and a "picture-thought" machine which described for us how we might open the canisters and seal the Cave entrance. We sat upon the floor and discussed that which we had seen and experienced. "Wonderful! Wonderful!" said a lama. "Don't see anything wonderful in it," said I, brashly. "We could have seen all that by looking at the Akashic Record. Why should we not look at those time-stream pictures and see what happened after this place was sealed up?" The others turned enquiringly to the senior of the party, the Lama Mingyar Dondup. He nodded slightly and remarked, "Sometimes our Lobsang shows glimmerings of intelligence! Let us compose ourselves and see what happened, for I am as curious as you." We sat in a rough circle, each facing in, and with our fingers interlocked in the appropriate pattern. My Guide started the necessary breathing rhythm and we all followed his lead. Slowly we lost our Earth identities and became as one floating in the Sea of Time. All that has ever happened can be seen by those who have the ability to consciously go into the astral and return—conscious—with the knowledge gained. Any scene in history, from an age no matter how remote, can be seen as if one were actually there.

I remembered the first time I had experienced the "Akashic Record." My Guide had been telling me about such things, and I had replied, "Yes, but what *is* it? How does it work? How *can* one get in touch with things that have passed, that are finished and gone?" "Lobsang!" he had replied, "you will agree that you have a memory. You can remember what happened yesterday, and the day before, and the day before that. With a little training you can remember everything that has happened in your life, you can, with training, remember even the process of being born. You can have what we term 'total recall' and that will take your memory back to *before* you were born. The Akashic Record is merely the 'memory' of the whole world. Everything that has ever happened on this Earth can be 'recalled' in just the same way as *you* can remember past events in your life. There is no magic involved, but we will deal with that and hypnotism—a closely related subject—at a later date."

With our training it was easy indeed to select the point at which the Machine had faded out its pictures. We saw the procession of men and women, notables of that time no doubt, file out of the Cave. Machines with vast arms slid what appeared to be half a mountain over the entrance. The cracks and crevices where surfaces met were carefully sealed, and the group of people and the workmen went away. Machines rolled into the distance and for a time, some months, the scene was quiet. We saw a high priest standing on the steps of an immense Pyramid, exhorting his listeners to war. The pictures impressed upon the Scrolls of Time rolled on, changed, and we saw the opposing camp. Saw the leaders ranting and raving. Time moved on. We saw streaks of white vapour in the blue of the skies, and then those skies turned red. The whole world trembled and shook. We, watching, experienced vertigo. The darkness of the night fell over the world. Black clouds, shot with vivid flames, rolled around the whole globe. Cities flamed briefly and were gone.

Across the land surged the raging seas. Sweeping all

before it, a giant wave, taller than the tallest building had been, roared across the land, its crest bearing aloft the flotsam of a dying civilization. The Earth shook and thundered in agony, great chasms appeared and closed again like the gaping maws of a giant. The mountains waved like willow twigs in a storm, waved, and sank beneath the seas. Land masses rose from the waters and became mountains. The whole surface of the world was in a state of change, of continuous motion. A few scattered survivors, out of millions, fled shrieking to the newly risen mountains. Others, afloat in ships that somehow survived the upheaval, reached the high ground and fled into any hiding place they could find. The Earth itself stood still, stopped its direction of rotation, and then turned in the opposite direction. Forests flashed from trees to scattered ash in the twinkling of an eye. The surface of the Earth was desolate, ruined, charred to a black crisp. Deep in holes, or in the lava-tunnels of extinct volcanoes, a scattered handful of Earth's population, driven insane by the catastrophe, cowered and gibbered in their terror. From the black skies fell a whitish substance, sweet to the taste, sustaining of life.

In the course of centuries the Earth changed again; the seas were now land, and the lands that had been were now seas. A low-lying plain had its rocky walls cracked and sundered, and the waters rushed in to form the Sea now known as the Mediterranean. Another sea nearby sank through a gap in the sea bed, and as the waters left and the bed dried, the Sahara Desert was formed. Over the face of the Earth wandered wild tribes who, by the light of their camp fires, told of the old legends, told of the Flood, of Lemuria, and Atlantis. They told, too, of the day the Sun Stood Still.

The Cave of the Ancients lay buried in the silt of a half-drowned world. Safe from intruders, it rested far beneath the surface of the land. In course of time, fast-running streams would wash away the silt, the debris, and allow the rocks to stand forth in the sunlight once more. At last, heated by the sun and cooled by a sudden icy shower, the rock face would split with thunderous noise and *we* would be able to enter.

We shook ourselves, stretched our cramped limbs, and rose wearily to our feet. The experience had been a shattering one. Now we had to eat, to sleep, and on the morrow we would look about us again so that we might perhaps learn something. Then, our mission accomplished, we would wall up the entrance as directed. The Cave would sleep again in peace until men of goodwill and high intelligence would come again. I wandered to the Cave mouth and looked down upon the desolation, upon the riven rocks, and I wondered what a man of the Old Times would think if he could rise from his grave to stand beside me, here.

As I turned in to the interior I marvelled at the contrast; a lama was lighting a fire with flint and tinder, igniting some dried yak dung which we had brought for that purpose. Around us were the machines and artifacts of a bygone age. We—modern men—were heating water over a dung fire, surrounded by such marvellous machines that they were beyond our comprehension. I sighed, and turned my thoughts to that of mixing tea and tsampa.

CHAPTER SIX

The mid-morning Service had ended; we boys rushed along to our classroom, shoving and pushing in an effort not to be the last one in. Not because of our interest in education, but because the Master at this class had the horrid habit of taking a swipe with his cane at the last one in! I, joy of joys, managed to be the *first* one in and basked in the glow of approval of the Master's smile. Impatiently he motioned the others to hurry, standing by the door and cuffing those who even appeared to be slow. At last we were all seated, sitting cross legged upon the seat-mats spread on the floor. As is our custom, we had our backs toward the Master, who constantly patrolled *behind* us so that we never knew where he was and thus we *had* to work hard.

"Today we will discuss how all religions are similar," he intoned. "We have observed how the story of the Flood is common to all beliefs throughout the world. Now we will give our attention to the theme of the Virgin Mother. Even the meanest intelligence," he said, looking hard at me, "knows that our Virgin Mother, the Blessed Dolma, the Virgin Mother of Mercy, corresponds to the Virgin Mother of certain sects of the Christian Faith." Hurrying footsteps stopped at the entrance of the classroom. A monk-messenger entered and bowed to the Master. "Salutations to you, Learned One," he murmured. "The Lord Lama Mingyar Dondup presents his compliments and requests that the boy Tuesday Lobsang Rampa be released from class *immediately*—the matter is urgent." The Master scowled; *"Boy!"* he thundered, "you are a nuisance and a disturber of the class, *get out*!" Hastily I jumped to my feet, bowed to the Master, and rushed after the hurrying Messenger. "What is it?" I gasped. "Don't know," he said, "wondered myself. Holy Lama Dondup has surgical things ready, horses ready too." We hurried on.

"Ah! Lobsang! So you *can* hurry!" laughed my Guide as we came upon him. "We are going down to the Village of Shö where our surgical services are required." He mounted his horse and motioned for me to mount mine. This was always a difficult operation; horses and I never seemed to be of one mind when it came to mounting. I walked toward the horse, and that creature walked sideways away from me. I slipped round to the other side and took a running jump before the horse knew what was happening. Then I tried to emulate mountain lichen with the tenacity of my grip. Snorting with exasperated resignation, the horse turned without help from me and followed the horse of my Guide down the path. This horse of mine had the horrible habit of stopping at the steepest parts and looking over the edge, lowering his head and doing a kind of shimmy. I firmly believe he had a (misplaced) sense of humour and was fully aware of the effect he had upon me. We clattered down the path and soon passed the Pargo Kaling, or Western Gate, and thus came upon the Village of Shö. My Guide led the way through the streets until he came to a big building which I recognized as the prison. Guards hurried out and took our horses. I picked up the two cases of my Guide the Lama Mingyar Dondup, and carried them into the gloomy place. This was unpleasant, a horrible spot indeed, I could *smell* the fear, *see* the evil thought-forms of wrong-doers. It was indeed a place the atmosphere of which made the hairs stand out upon the back of my neck.

I followed my Guide into a fairly large room. The sunlight was streaming through the windows. A number of guards were standing about, and waiting to greet the Lama Mingyar Dondup was a Magistrate of Shö. While they talked I looked about me. This, I decided, was where criminals were tried and sentenced. Around the walls were records and books. On the floor, to one side, was a groaning bundle. I looked toward it, and at the same time heard the Magistrate talking to my Guide; "Chinese, a spy we think, Honourable Lama. He was trying to climb the Holy Mountain, apparently trying to creep into the Potala. He slipped and fell. How far? Perhaps a hundred feet. He is in a bad way." My Guide moved forward, and I went to his side. A man pulled back the covers and before us we saw a Chinese man, of about middle age. He was fairly small and looked as though he had been remarkably agile —something like an acrobat—I thought. Now he was groaning with pain, his face wet with perspiration, and his complexion of a muddy greenish tinge.

The man was in a bad state, shivering and grinding his teeth in his agony. The Lama Mingyar Dondup looked at him with compassion. "Spy, would-be assassin, or whatever he is, we must do something for him," he said. My Guide knelt beside the man and put his hands on the suffering wretch's temples and gazed into his eyes. Within seconds the sick man relaxed, eyes half open, a vague smile on his lips. My Guide pulled the coverings further aside then bent over his legs. I felt sick at what I saw; the man's leg bones protruding through his trousers. The legs appeared to be completely shattered. With a sharp knife my Guide cut off the man's clothing. There was a gasp from the onlookers as they saw the legs with bones completely shattered from feet to thighs. The Lama gently felt them. The injured man did not stir or flinch, he was deeply hypnotised. The leg bones grated and sounded like half-filled sand bags. "The bones are too shattered to set," said my Guide. "his legs seem to be pulverised; we shall have to amputate them." "Honourable Lama," said the Magistrate, "can you make him tell us what he was doing? We fear he was an assassin." "We will remove his legs first," replied the Lama, "*then* we can ask him." He bent over the man again and gazed once more into his eyes. The Chinese relaxed even more and appeared to go into a deep sleep.

100

I had the bags unrolled and the sterilising herbal fluid ready in the bowl. My Guide dipped in his hands so that they could soak. I had his instruments already in another bowl. At his direction I washed the man's body and legs. Touching those legs sent a peculiar feeling through me; it felt as though *everything* was shattered. Now they were a blue, mottled colour, with the veins standing out like black cords. Under the direction of my Guide, who was still soaking his hands, I placed sterilised bands as high as I could on the Chinese man's legs, high, where they joined the body. Sliding a stick into a loop I turned until the pressure stopped the circulation. Very quickly the Lama Mingyar Dondup seized a knife and cut the flesh in a vee. At the point of the vee he sawed through the leg bone—what was left of it—and then tucked in the two flaps of the vee so that the end of the bone was protected by a double layer of flesh. I passed him thread made from the sterilised parts of a yak, and speedily he stitched the flaps tightly together. Slowly, carefully I eased the pressure of the band about the man's leg, ready to tighten again should the stump bleed. The stitches held, no blood flowed. Behind us a guard retched violently, turned chalk white and fell to the floor in a faint!

Carefully my Guide bandaged the stump and again washed his hands in the solution. I gave my attention to the other leg, the left, and slid the stick through the loop in the band. The Lama nodded, and I turned the stick once more to shut off the blood from that leg. Soon that limb was lying beside the other. My Guide turned to a staring guard and told him to take the legs and wrap them up in cloth. "We must return these legs to the Chinese Mission," said the Lama, "or they will say that their man has been tortured. I shall ask the Inmost One that this man be returned to his people. His mission does not matter; it failed as all such attempts will." "But Honourable Lama!" said the Magistrate, "The man should be *forced* to tell what he was doing, and why." My Guide said nothing, but turned again to the hypnotised man and looked deeply into his now-opened eyes. "What were you doing?" he asked. The man groaned and rolled his eyes. My Guide asked him again; "What were you going to do? Were you going to assassinate a High Person with the Potala?" Froth formed around the Chinese man's mouth then, reluctantly, he nodded his head in confirmation. *"Speak!"* commanded the Lama. "A nod is not enough." So, slowly, painfully, the story came out. An assassin paid to do murder, paid to stir up trouble in a peaceful country. An assassin who had failed, as all would fail, through not knowing of *our* safety devices! As I was musing upon this the Lama Mingyar Dondup rose to his feet. "I will go to see the Inmost One, Lobsang, you stay here and guard this man," he said.

The man groaned. "You kill me?" he asked weakly. "No!" I replied, "we kill no one." I moistened his lips and mopped his brow. Soon he was still again; I think he slept after the exhausting ordeal. The Magistrate looked on sourly, thinking that priests were crazy to want to save a would-be assassin. The day dragged on. Guards went and others came. I felt my interior rumble with hunger. At last I heard familiar footsteps, and the Lama Mingyar Dondup strode into the room. First he came and looked at the patient, making sure that the man was as comfortable as the circumstances permitted and that the stumps were not bleeding. Rising to his feet, he looked at the senior lay official, and said, "By virtue of the authority vested in me by the Inmost One I command you to obtain two litters, immediately, and take this man and his legs to the Chinese Mission." He turned to me; "You will accompany these men and report to me if they are unnecessarily rough in their handling of the man's litter." I felt distinctly gloomy; here was this assassin with his legs cut off—and my stomach rumbling away as empty of food as a temple drum. While the men were absent in search of litters I rushed outside to where I had seen the officials drinking tea! In a haughty voice I demanded—and got—a generous helping. Hastily cramming tsampa down my throat, I rushed back.

Silently, sullenly, the men filed into the room after me, carrying two rough litters, cloth stretched between the poles. Grumpily they picked up the two legs and put them on one litter. Gently, under the keen eyes of the Lama Mingyar Dondup, they placed the Chinese man upon the other litter. A cover was placed over his body and tied under the litter so that he could not be jolted off. My Guide turned to the senior lay official and said, "You will accompany these men and you will present my compliments to the Chinese Ambassador and tell him we are returning one of his men. You, Lobsang," he turned to me, "will accompany them and on your return you will report to me." He turned away, and the men trudged out of the room. The air was chilly outside and I shivered in my light robe. Down the Mani Lhakhang we trudged, the men carrying the legs first, then the two men carrying the litter with the Chinaman. I walked to one side and the senior lay official walked on the other. We turned off to the right, passed the two Parks and headed on towards the Chinese Mission.

With the Happy River glinting ahead of us, showing flecks of bright light through gaps in the trees, we came to the farthermost wall of the Mission. Grunting, the men put down their loads for a time while they rested their aching muscles and looked curiously at the Mission wall. The Chinese were *very* offensive to any who tried to intrude on their ground. There had been cases of small boys being shot "by accident" when they trespassed as small boys will. Now we were going inside! Spitting on their hands, the men stooped and picked up the litters again. Marching on we turned left into the Lingkor Road and entered the Mission grounds. Surly men came to the door and the senior official said, "I have the honour to return to you one of your men who attempted to stray into Holy Ground. He fell and his legs had to be amputated. Here are the legs for your inspection." Scowling guards seized the handles and rushed into the building with the man and his legs. Others, at gunpoint, waved us away. We retreated

103

down the path. I slipped unseen behind a tree. The others marched on. Screams and shouts rent the air. Looking about, I saw that there were no guards; they had all entered the Mission. On a foolish impulse, I left the doubtful security of the tree and ran silently to the window. The injured man was lying on the floor, one guard was sitting on his chest, while two more sat on his arms. A fourth man was applying burning cigarettes to his amputated stumps. Suddenly the fourth man jumped to his feet, drew his revolver and shot the injured man between the eyes.

A twig cracked behind me. Like a flash I dropped to my knees and turned about. Another Chinese guard had appeared and was aiming a rifle at where my head had been. I dived between his legs, tripping him and causing him to drop his rifle. Hastily I ran from tree to tree. Shots came ripping through the low branches and there was the thud of running feet behind me. Here the advantage was wholly mine; I was fleet of foot and the Chinaman stopped often to take shots at me. I rushed to the back of the garden—the gate was now guarded—climbed up a convenient tree and inched along a branch so that I could drop on to the top of the wall. Seconds later I was back on the road *ahead* of my countrymen who had carried in the injured man. As soon as they heard my story they hurried up their footsteps. No longer were they tarrying in the hope of seeing some excitement; now they wanted to avoid it. A Chinese guard dropped off the top of the wall onto the road and glared at me most suspiciously. I blandly gazed back at him. With a scowl and a muttered oath which reflected adversely on my parentage he turned away. We put on speed!

Back at the Village of Shö the men left me. Looking somewhat apprehensively over my shoulder, I hurried on and soon was speeding up the path to Chakpori. An old monk resting by the wayside called after me, "What is wrong with you, Lobsang? You look as if all the Demons were after you!" I rushed on and, breathless, entered the room of my Guide, the Lama Mingyar Dondup. For a moment I stood panting, trying to get my breath. "Ow!"

I gasped at last, "The Chinese murdered that man; they *shot* him!" In a torrent of words I told all that had happened. My Guide was silent for a moment. Then he said, "You will see much violence in your life, Lobsang, so do not be too distressed at this event. This is the usual method of diplomacy; kill those who fail and disclaim spies who are caught. It goes on all over the world, in all countries of the world."

Sitting in front of my Guide, recovering in the calm serenity of his presence, I thought of another matter which was troubling me. "Sir!" I exclaimed, "How does hypnotism work?" He looked across at me with a smile on his lips. "When did you eat last?" he queried. With a rush all my hunger came back. "Oh, about twelve hours ago," I replied somewhat ruefully. "Then let us eat now, here, and then when we are somewhat refreshed we can discuss hypnotism." He waved me to silence, and sat in the attitude of meditation. I caught his telepathic message to his servants—*food* and tea. I caught too a telepathic message to someone at the Potala, someone who had to go to the Inmost One in a hurry to give a detailed report. But my "interception" of the telepathic message was interrupted by the entry of a servant bringing food and tea. . . . !

I sat back, replete with food, feeling even more uncomfortably full. I *had* had a hard day, I *had* been hungry for many, many hours, but (the thought troubled me internally) had I eaten too much too unwisely now? Suddenly, suspiciously, I looked up. My Guide was gazing down upon me with obvious amusement on his face. "Yes, Lobsang," he remarked, "you *have* eaten too much. I hope you will be able to follow my talk on hypnotism." He studied my flushed face and his own look softened. "Poor Lobsang, you have had a hard day. Go to your rest now and we will continue our discussion on the morrow." He rose to his feet and left the room. I climbed wearily to mine and almost tottered along the corridor. Sleep! That was all I wanted. Food? Pfaugh! I had had too much of that. I reached my bedplace and rolled myself in my robes.

Sleep was troubled indeed; I had nightmares in which legless Chinese chased me through wooded groves and other Chinese armed with guns kept jumping on my shoulders in an attempt to bring me down.

"Thump!" went my head on the ground. One of the Chinese guards was kicking me. *"Thump!"* went my head again. Blearily I opened my eyes to find an acolyte energetically banging my head and kicking me in a desperate attempt to wake me. "Lobsang!" he exclaimed as he saw that my eyes were open. "Lobsang, I thought you were dead. You have slept all through the night, missed the Services, and only the intervention of your Master, the Lama Mingyar Dondup, has saved you from the Proctors. *Wake up!*" he shouted, as I almost lapsed into sleep again.

Consciousness flooded into me. Through the windows I saw the early morning rays of sunlight peering over the high Himalayas and lighting up the tallest buildings in the valley, showing the golden roofs of the distant Sera, glowing along the top of the Pargo Kaling. Yesterday I had gone to the Village of Shö—ah! *that* was not a dream. Today, today I *hoped* to miss some lessons and learn direct from my beloved Mingyar Dondup. Learn about Hypnotism, too! Soon I had finished my breakfast and was on my way to the classroom, not to stay and recite from the hundred and eight Sacred Books, but to explain why I was not!

"Sir!" I said, as I saw the Teacher just going into the classroom, "Sir! I have to attend the Lama Mingyar Dondup this day. I beg to be excused from class." "Ah, yes! my boy," said the Teacher in amazingly genial tones. "I have had a word with the Holy Lama your Guide. He was good enough to comment favourably upon your progress under my care; I confess I am most gratified, *most* gratified." Astonishingly, he extended his hand and patted me upon the shoulder before entering the classroom. Bemused, and wondering what sort of magic had been worked upon him, I wandered off towards the Lamas' Quarters.

On I strolled without a care in the world. Past a half-opened doorway. *"Ow!"* I exclaimed suddenly, coming to a sudden stop. *"Pickled walnuts!!"* The scent of them was strong. Back-tracking silently, I peered through the doorway. An old monk was staring down at the stone floor, muttering things which were not his prayers, mourning the loss of a whole jar of pickled walnuts which had somehow been obtained from India. "May I help you, Reverend Lama?" I asked politely. The old man turned a ferocious face to me and made such a rejoinder that I raced off along the corridor while I was still able. "All those words just for a few walnuts!" I said disgustedly to myself.

"Come in!" said my Guide as I approached his door. "I thought you had gone back to sleep." "Sir!" I said, "I have come to you for instruction. I am anxious to know the nature of hypnotism." "Lobsang," said my Guide, "you have to learn much more than that. You have to learn the basis for hypnotism first. Otherwise you do not know exactly what you do. Sit down." I sat, cross legged of course, upon the floor. My Guide sat opposite me. For a time he seemed lost in thought, and then said: "By now you should have realised that everything is vibration, electricity. The body has many different chemicals in its composition. Certain of those chemicals are conveyed to the brain by the blood stream. The brain, you know, has the best supply of blood and its contained chemicals. Those ingredients, potassium, manganese, carbon, and many others, form the brain tissue. Interaction between them makes a peculiar oscillation of molecules which we term an 'electric current.' When one *thinks* one sets in motion a chain of circumstances which results in the formation of this electric current and, hence, 'brain waves'."

I pondered the whole matter; I could not see all this. If there were "electric currents" in my brain, why did I not feel the shock? That boy who was flying a kite, I recalled, had been doing so in a thunderstorm. I remembered the vivid blue flash as lightning travelled along his wet kite line; I remembered, with a shudder, how he had fallen to the ground as a dried-up, fried crisp of flesh. And once I too had had a shock from the same source, a mere tingle compared to the other, but "tingle" enough to throw me a dozen feet.

"Honourable Lama!" I expostulated, "how *can* there be electricity in the brain? It would drive a man mad with the pain!" My Guide sat and laughed at me. "Lobsang!" he chuckled, "the shock you once had has given you a wholly incorrect idea of electricity. The amount of electricity in the brain is of a very small order indeed. Delicate instruments can measure it and can actually chart the variations as one thinks or undertakes some physical action." The thought of one man measuring another man's voltage was almost too much for me, I started to laugh. My Guide merely smiled and said: "Let us this afternoon walk over to the Potala. The Inmost One has there a device which will enable us to talk more easily on this electrical subject. Go now and entertain yourself—have a meal, put on your best robe and meet me here when the sun is at noon." I rose to my feet, bowed, and went out.

For two hours I wandered around, climbing to the roof and idly flicking small pebbles on to the unsuspecting heads of monks passing below. Tiring of that sport, I lowered myself head first through a trap-hatch leading down to a dark corridor. Hanging upside down by my feet I was just in time to hear approaching footsteps. I could not see, because the trap-hatch was at a corner. Sticking out my tongue, and making a ferocious face, I waited. An old man came round the corner and, not being able to see me, bumped into me. My wet tongue touched his cheek. He emitted a shriek, and dropping the tray he was carrying with a *crash*, he disappeared at a speed surprising in such an old man. I too had a surprise; as the old monk bumped into me it dislodged my feet from their precarious hold. I fell on my back into the corridor. The trap-hatch fell with a resounding *crash* and a whole load of choking dust fell on top of me! Scrambling dizzily to my feet I made off as fast as I could in the opposite direction. Still suffering from the shock, I changed my robe and

108

had a meal; I was not shocked enough to forget *that!* Punctually, as the shadows vanished, and the day was at noon, I presented myself before my Guide. With some effort he composed his features as he saw me. "An elderly monk, Lobsang, swears that he was beset by a devil in the North corridor. A party of three lamas has gone there to exorcise the devil. No doubt I shall be doing my part if I take him—you—to the Potala as arranged. Come!" He turned and walked out of the room. I followed behind, casting apprehensive glances about me. After all, one never knew for sure what would happen if the Lamas were exorcising. I had vague visions of finding myself flying through the air to some unknown, probably uncomfortable, destination.

Out we went, into the open. Two ponies were being held by grooms. The Lama Mingyar Dondup mounted and slowly rode off down the mountain. I was helped on to my pony, and one of the grooms playfully gave him a slap. The pony felt playful too. Down went his head. Up went his rear, and off his back in an arc went I. A groom again held the animal while I picked myself from the ground and brushed off some of the dust. Then I mounted again, watching warily in case the grooms tried anything else.

That pony *knew* he had a duffer aboard; the moronic animal kept walking to the most dangerous places and stopping on the very edge. Then he would lower his head and gaze earnestly at the rocky ground so far below. At last I dismounted and towed the pony behind me. It was quicker. At the bottom of Iron Mountain I again mounted and followed my Guide into the Village of Shö. He had some business there which detained us for a few moments. Time enough for me to regain my breath and my shattered composure. Then, mounting again, we climbed up the broad, stepped Way to the Potala. Gladly I relinquished my pony to the waiting grooms. Even more gladly I followed the Lama Mingyar Dondup to his own apartment. My pleasure was increased by the knowledge that I should be staying here for a day or so.

Soon it was time to attend the service in the Temple below. Here at the Potala, services were—I thought—excessively formal, the discipline too strict. Having had more than enough of excitement for one day, as well as suffering from many small bruises, I remained on my best behaviour and the service was concluded without incident. It was now an accepted thing that when my Guide was at the Potala I should occupy a small room adjoining his. I went there and sat down to await events, knowing that the Lama Mingyar Dondup was engaged in matters of State with a very senior official who had recently returned from India. It was fascinating to look out of the window and see the City of Lhasa in the distance. The view was one of surpassing beauty; willow fringed lakes, golden gleams from the Jo Kang, and the milling throng of pilgrims who clamoured at the foot of the Holy Mountain in the hope of seeing the Inmost One (who was in residence) or at least some high official. An interminable string of traders and their beasts were just wending their slow way past the Pargo Kaling. I dwelt for a moment upon their exotic loads, but was interrupted by a soft footstep behind me.

"We will have tea, Lobsang, and then we will continue with our talk," said my Guide who had just entered. I followed him to his room where was laid out fare very different from that normally served to a poor monk. Tea, of course, but sweet things from India too. It was all *very* much to my taste. Normally monks never talk when they eat; it is considered to be disrespectful to the food, but on this occasion my Guide told me that the Russians were attempting to make trouble for Tibet, were attempting to infiltrate spies. Soon we finished our meal and then made our way to the rooms where the Dalai Lama stored many strange devices from far-off lands. For a time we just looked about us, the Lama Mingyar Dondup pointing out odd objects and explaining their uses. At last he stopped in a corner of one room and said, "Look at this, Lobsang!" I moved to his side and was not at all impressed with what I saw.

Before me, on a small table, stood a glass jar. Inside there depended two thin threads, each supporting at their far end a small sphere of something that appeared to be pith from a willow tree. "It *is* pith!" commented my Guide dryly, when I remarked upon the matter. "You, Lobsang," said the Lama, "think of electricity as something that gives you a shock. There is another kind, or manifestation, which we term static electricity. Now watch!"

From the table the Lama Mingyar Dondup took a shiny rod, possibly about twelve to fourteen inches long. Briskly he rubbed the rod on his robe and then brought it close to the glass jar. To my intense surprise the two pith spheres flew violently apart—and *stayed* apart even when the rod was withdrawn. "Keep watching!" exhorted my Guide. Well, that is what I was doing. After some minutes the pith balls slowly sank down again under the normal pull of gravity. Soon they were hanging straight down as they had before the experiment.

"You try it," commanded the Lama, extending the black rod to me. "By the Blessed Dolma!" I cried, "I'm *not touching that thing!*" My Guide laughed heartily at my more-than-distressed expression. "Try it, Lobsang," he said mildly, "for I have never played a trick on you yet." "Yes," I grumbled, "but there is always a first time." He pressed the rod upon me. Gingerly I took the awful object. Reluctantly, half-heartedly (expecting a shock at any moment) I rubbed the rod on my robe. There was no sensation, no shock or tingle. At last I held it toward the glass jar and—wonder of wonders!—*the pith balls flew apart again.* "As you observe, Lobsang," remarked my Guide, "electricity is flowing, yet even you feel no shock. Such is the electricity of the brain. Come with me."

He led me to another table upon which rested a most remarkable device. It appeared to be a wheel upon whose surface there were innumerable metal plates. Two rods were fixed so that a spray of wires from each lightly touched two of the metal plates. From the rods wires

111

trailed to two metal spheres which were about a foot apart. The thing made no sense at all to me. "Statue of a devil," I thought. My Guide confirmed that impression by his next move. Grasping a handle which projected from the back of the wheel he gave it a very hearty twirl. With a growl of rage the wheel sprang to life; flashing and winking. From the metal spheres a great tongue of blue lightning leaped, hissing and crackling. There was a strange smell as if the air itself were burning. I waited no longer; this most definitely was *not* the place for me. I dived beneath the biggest table and tried to wriggle my way to the far distant door.

The hissing and crackling stopped, to be replaced by another sound. I checked my flight and listened in amazement, was it the sound of *laughter*? Never! Nervously I peered from my sanctuary. There was the Lama Mingyar Dondup almost doubled up with laughter. Tears of merriment were trickling from his eyes, while his face was red with amusement. He seemed to be gasping for breath, too. "Oh, Lobsang!" he said at last, "that is the first time I have known anyone to be frightened of a Wimshurst Machine. These devices are used in many foreign countries that the properties of electricity may be demonstrated."

I crept out, feeling rather silly, and had a closer look at the strange machine. The Lama said, "I will hold these two wires, Lobsang, and you turn the handle as fast as you can. You will see lightning flash all over me, but it will not harm me nor cause me pain. Let us try. Who knows? Perhaps *you* will have an opportunity to laugh at *me!*" He took two wires, one in each hand, and nodded for me to start. Grimly I seized the handle and turned as fast as I could. I shouted in amazement as great purple and violet bands of lightning streamed across my Guide's hands and face. He was quite unperturbed. Meanwhile the smell had started again. "Ozone, quite harmless," said my Guide.

At last I was persuaded to hold the wires with the Lama turning the handle. The hissing and crackling was fearsome in the extreme, but as for feeling—it was more like a cool breeze than anything else! The Lama took various glass things from a box and one by one connected them to the machine by wires. As he turned the handle I saw a bright flame burning inside a glass bottle, and, in other bottles, a cross and other metal shapes outlined by living fire. But nowhere could I get a feeling of electric shock. With this Wimshurst Machine my Guide demonstrated how a person who was not clairvoyant could be enabled to see the human aura, but more of that later.

Eventually, the fading light caused us to desist from our experiments and to return to the Lama's room. First there was the evening service again, our life in Tibet seemed to be completely circumscribed by the needs for religious observance. With the service behind us we returned once again to my Guide the Lama Mingyar Dondup's apartment, here we sat in our usual cross legged attitude upon the floor with the little table, perhaps fourteen inches high, between us.

"Now Lobsang," said my Guide, "we have to get down to this matter of hypnotism, but first of all we have to decide upon the operation of the human brain. I have shown you—I hope!—that there can be the passage of an electric current without one experiencing pain or discomfort therefrom. Now, I want you to consider that when a person thinks he generates an electric current. We need not go into the matter of how an electric current stimulates muscle fibre and causes reaction, our whole interest for the moment is the electric current—the brain waves which have been so clearly measured and charted by Western medical science." I confess that I found this to be of some interest to me because in my small and humble way it had already occurred to me that thought had force, because I remembered that parchment roughly perforated cylinder which I had used at times in the Lamasery, and which I had caused to rotate by thought power alone.

"Your attention is wandering, Lobsang!" said my Guide. "I am sorry, Honourable Master," I replied, "I was merely reflecting upon the undoubted nature of thought waves, and considering the amusement I derived from that cylinder to which you introduced me some months ago."

My Guide looked at me and said, "You are an entity, an individual, and you have your own thoughts. You may consider that you will do some course of action, such as lift that rosary. Even in considering an action your brain causes electricity to flow from its chemical constitutents, and the wave from the electricity prepares your muscle for the impending action. If a greater electrical force should occur in your brain, then your original intention of lifting that rosary would be thwarted. It is easy to see that if I can persuade you that you cannot lift that rosary, then your brain—being beyond your immediate control—will generate and send out an opposing wave. You will then be unable to lift the rosary or do the contemplated action." I looked at him, and thought of the affair, and it really did not make much sense to me, for how could he influence how much electricity my brain was generating? I thought about it, and looked at him, and wondered if I should voice my doubt. There was no necessity to, however, for he divined it and hastened to set my mind at rest. "I can assure you, Lobsang, that what I say is demonstrable fact, and in a Western country we should be able to prove all this under a piece of apparatus which would chart the three basic brain waves, here however, we have no such facilities and we can only debate the matter. The brain generates electricity, it generates waves, and if you decide to lift your arm then your brain generates waves on the intention of your decision. If I can —in rather technical words—feed a negative charge into your brain, then your original intention would be frustrated. In other words, you would be hypnotised!"

This really did begin to make sense; I had seen that Wimshurst Machine, and I had seen various demonstrations conducted with its assistance, and I had seen how it was possible to alter the polarity of a current and so

114

cause it to flow in the opposite direction. "Honourable Lama," I exclaimed, "how is it possible for you to feed a current into my brain? You cannot take off the top of my head and put some electricity inside, how then may it be done?" "My dear Lobsang," said my Guide, "it is not necessary to get into your head because I do not have to generate any electricity and put it into you. I can make appropriate suggestions whereby you will be convinced of the accuracy of my statement or suggestions, and you will then—without any voluntary control on your part—generate that negative current yourself."

He looked at me and said, "I am most unwilling to hypnotise anyone against their will except in a case of medical or surgical necessity, but I think that with your co-operation it might be a good idea to demonstrate a simple little matter of hypnotism." I exclaimed hastily, "Oh yes, I should love to experience hypnotism!" He rather smiled at my impetuosity and asked, "Now, Lobsang, what would you be unwilling to do, normally? I ask you that because I want to hypnotise you into doing something that you would not willingly do so that you personally can be assured that in doing this thing you are acting under involuntary influence!" I thought for a moment, and really I hardly knew what to say, there were so many things that I did not want to do! I was, saved further thought on this matter by my Guide, who exclaimed, "I know! You were not at all anxious to read that rather involved passage in the fifth volume of the Kangyur. You were, I believe, rather afraid that some of the terms used would betray you, and betray the fact that on that particular subject you had not studied so assiduously as desired by your tutor!"

I felt rather gloomy about that, and I confess I also felt my cheeks redden with some embarrassment. It was perfectly true, there was a particularly difficult passage in The Book which caused me extreme difficulty, however, in the interests of science I was quite prepared to be persuaded to read it. Actually I had almost a phobia against

115

reading that particular passage! My Guide smiled and said, "The Book is over there just to the side of the window, bring it here, turn to that passage and read it aloud, and if you will try not to read it—if you will try to mess up the whole thing—then that will be a much better test." I reluctantly went across and fetched The Book, and unwillingly turned over the pages. Our Tibetan pages are much bigger—much heavier—than Western books. I fumbled and fumbled, and made the thing as long-drawn-out as possible. In the end, though, I turned to the appropriate passage, and I confess that this particular passage, because of some earlier incident with a tutor, really did make me feel almost physically sick.

I stood there with The Book in front of me, and try as I might I could not articulate those words, it may seem strange but it is a fact that because I had been so ill-used by an un-understanding tutor I had developed a real hatred for those sacred sentences. My Guide looked at me—nothing more—just looked at me, and then something seemed to click inside my head, and I found to my very considerable surprise that I was reading, not just "reading" but reading fluently, easily, without a trace of hesitation. As I reached the end of the paragraph I had the most inexplicable sensation. I put down The Book and I went to the middle of the room and I stood on my head! "I'm going crazy!" I thought. "Whatever will my Guide think of me for behaving in this utterly foolish manner?" Then it occurred to me, that my Guide was making me—influencing me—to behave thus. Quickly I jumped to my feet, and found that he was smiling most benevolently upon me. "It really is a most easy matter, Lobsang, to influence a person, there is no difficulty at all when one has mastered the basic matter. I merely thought of certain things and you picked up my thoughts telepathically, and that caused your brain to react in the manner I had anticipated. Thus certain fluctuations in your normal brain pattern were caused which produced this quite interesting result!"

"Honourable Lama!" I said, "then does it mean that if we can put an electric current into a person's brain we can make that person do anythng we want?" "No, it does not mean that at all," said my Guide. "It means instead that if we can persuade a person to do a certain course of action, and the course of action which we desire to persuade is not contrary to that person's belief, then he will undoubtedly do it merely because his brain waves have been altered, and no matter what his original intention, he will react as suggested by the hypnotist. In most cases a person receives suggestions from a hypnotist, there is no real influence exerted by the hypnotist other than the influence of suggestion. The hypnotist, by certain little tricks is able to induce a course of action in the victim contrary to that which was originally contemplated." He looked at me seriously for a moment and then added, "Of course you and I have other powers than that. You will be able to hypnotise a person instantly even against a person's wishes, that gift is being made unto you because of the peculiar nature of your life, because of the very great hardships, because of the exceptional work which you are going to have to achieve."

He sat back and gazed at me in order that he might determine if I had assimilated the information which he had given me, satisfied that I had, he continued, "Later —not yet—you will be taught much more about hypnotism and how to hypnotise quickly. I want to tell you that you will also have your telepathic powers increased, because when you journey from here far out into other countries you will need to keep in touch with us all the time, and the quickest and the most accurate way is by telepathy." I felt quite gloomy over all this. I seemed the whole time to be learning something fresh, and the more I learned the less time I had for myself, it seemed to me that more and more work was being added to me but none was being lifted off!

"But, Honourable Lama!" I said, "how does telepathy work? Nothing appears to happen between us, yet you know almost everything I think especially when I do not want you to!" My Guide looked at me and laughed, and said, "It really is quite a simple matter, telepathy, one merely has to control the brain waves. Look at it in this way; you think, your brain generates electric currents which fluctuate in accordance with the variations of your thought. Normally your thoughts go to activate a muscle so that a limb may be raised or lowered, or you may be thinking of a certain subject at a distance, whatever way it is, your mental energy is broadcast—that is, the energy-force from your brain is emitted indiscriminately in each and every direction. If there were some method whereby you could focus your thought, then it would be of a very much greater intensity in the direction in which it was focused." I looked at him, and I remembered a little experiment which he had shown me some time before; we had been in much the same position as now, that is high up on The Peak (as we Tibetans call the Potala). The Lama, my Guide, had in the darkness of the night lighted a small candle and the light glimmered faintly around. But then he had put a magnifying glass in front of the candle, and by adjusting the distance of the magnifying glass from the flame he had been able to project upon the wall a much brighter image of the candle flame. To increase the lesson, he had put a shiny surface behind the candle, and that, in turn, had concentrated the light more so that the image upon the wall was even greater. I mentioned this to him, and he said, "Yes! That is perfectly correct, by various tricks it is possible to focus the thought and to send it in a certain predetermined direction. Actually, every person has what we might term an individual wave-length, that is, the amount of energy on the basic wave emitted from the brain of any one person follows a precise order of oscillation, and if we could determine the rate of oscillation of the basic brain wave of another person and tune in to that basic oscillation, we should have no difficulty whatever in conveying our message by so-called telepathy, irrespective of the distance." He gazed firmly at me, and added, "You must get it quite clear in your mind, Lobsang, that distance means nothing whatever when it comes to telepathy, telepathy can span oceans, it can even span worlds!"

I confess that I was most anxious to do more in the realm of telepathy, I could visualise myself talking to those of my fellows who were at other lamaseries, such as Sera, or even in far-off districts. It seemed to me, though, that all my efforts had to be devoted to things which would help me in the future, a future—which, according to all prophecies, would be a gloomy affair indeed.

My Guide interrupted my thoughts again, "We will go into this matter of telepathy later. We will also go into the matter of clairvoyance, for you will have abnormal powers of clairvoyance, and it will ease things for you if you are aware of the mechanics of the process. It all revolves around brain waves and interrupting the Akashic Record, but night is upon us, we must cease our discussion for the moment and prepare for sleep that we may during the night hours be refreshed in time for the first service."

He rose to his feet, and I rose to mine. I bowed to him in the attitude of respect, and I wished that I could show more adequately the profound respect which I felt for this great man who had so befriended me.

Briefly, a fleeting smile crossed his lips, and he stepped forward and I felt his warm handclasp upon my shoulder. A gentle pat, and he said, "Goodnight, Lobsang, we must not delay any longer, or we shall be logheads again—unable to awaken when it is time for us to attend to our devotions."

In my own room I stood for some moments by the window with the cold night air blowing in. I gazed out upon the lights of Lhasa, and reflected upon all that had been told to me, and upon all that I had yet to learn. It was obvious to me that the more I learned, the more there was to learn, and I wondered where it would all end. With a sigh, perhaps of despair, I rolled myself more tightly in my robe and lay down upon the cold floor to sleep.

CHAPTER SEVEN

A cold cold wind was blowing down off the mountains. Dust and small stones whipped through the air and most of them seemed to aim directly for our shrinking bodies. Wise old animals stood with bowed head to wind that their fur should not be disturbed and cause them to lose body heat. We rounded the corner from the Kundu Ling and turned into the Mani Lhakhang. A sudden blast of air, even fiercer than the others, swept under the robes of one of my companions, and with a howl of fright he was blown up into the air like a kite. We looked up, awestruck, with our mouths open. He appeared to be flying to the City—arms outstretched, robes billowing and making him into giant size. Then there came a lull, and he dropped like a stone into the Kaling Chu! We rushed madly to the scene, fearing he would drown. As we reached the bank he—Yulgye—seemed to be standing knee deep in the water. The gale shrieked with renewed force, swirling Yulgye around and sweeping him backwards to our arms. Wonder of wonders, he was hardly wet, except from the knees down. We hastened away, holding our robes tightly to us lest we too be blown into the air.

Along the Mani Lhakhang we marched. And an easy march it was! The howling gale blew us along; our only effort was to maintain a vertical position! In the Village of Shö a party of high ranking ladies was seeking shelter; I always liked to guess at the identity of the person behind the leather face mask. The "younger" the face painted on the leather the *older* the woman who wore it. Tibet is a cruel and harsh country, with screaming winds blowing torrents of stones and sand from the mountains. Men and women often wore masks made of leather as protection from the storms. These masks, with slits for eyes and another slit through which one breathed, were invariably painted with a representation of the wearer's opinion of herself!

"Let's go by The Street of Shops!" yelled Timon, striving to make himself heard above the gale. "Waste of time," screamed Yulgye, "they put up the shutters when there is a gale like this. All their stock would be blown away otherwise." We hurried on, going at more than twice our normal pace. Crossing by the Turquoise Bridge we had to hold on to each other, the force of the wind was so great. Looking back, we saw that the Potala and Iron Mountain were obscured by a black sullen cloud. A cloud composed of dust particles and small stones worn and torn from the eternal Himalayas. Hurrying on, knowing that the black cloud would overtake us if we were laggard, we passed the House of Doring just outside the Inner Circle around the immense Jo Kang. With a roar the storm was upon us, beating at our unprotected heads and faces. Timon instinctively raised his hands to protect his eyes. The wind gripped his robe and raised it high over his head, leaving him as bare as a peeled banana, just before the Cathedral of Lhasa.

Stones and twigs came bowling down the street towards us, bruising our legs and, at times, drawing blood. The sky became blacker, as dark as night. Hustling Timon before us, struggling with the flapping robe which swirled around his head, we staggered into the Sanctuary of the Holy Place. Inside was *peace,* profound peace, soothing peace. Here, for some thirteen hundred years, had come the devout to worship. Even the fabric of the building exuded sanctity. The stone floor was ribbed and grooved by the passage of generation after generation of pilgrims. The air felt alive, so much incense had been burned here throughout the ages that it seemed to have endowed the place with a sentient life of its own.

Age-blackened pillars and beams loomed through the perpetual dusk. The dull glitter of gold, reflecting the light of butter lamps and candles did little to bring a lightening of the gloom. The little flickering flames turned the shadows of the Sacred Figures into a grotesque dance on the Temple walls. God cavorted with Goddess in a never ending play of light and shadow as the endless procession of devout pilgrims moved past the lamps.

Pin-points of light of all colours shot forth from the great heaps of jewels. Diamonds, topaz, beryl, rubies and jade flashed forth the light of their nature, forming an everchanging pattern, a kaleidoscope of colour. Great openwork iron nets, with links just too small to permit the passage of a hand, guarded the gems and gold from those whose cupidity overcame their rectitude. Here and there, in the brilliant dusk behind the iron curtain, pairs of red eyes gleamed, proof that the Temple cats were ever on the alert. Incorruptible, unbribable without fear of Man or beast, they padded silently on velvet paws. But those soft feet held sheathed claws of razor-sharpness should their ire be aroused. Of surpassing intelligence, they had but to look at one to know one's intentions. A suspicious move toward the jewels they guarded, and they would become devils incarnate; working in pairs one would flash at the throat of the would-be thief while the other would cling to his right arm. Only death would loose their grip unless the attending monks came quickly.

To me, or to others like me who loved them, the cats would roll and purr, and permit us to play with the priceless gems. Play, but not to take away. All black, with vivid blue eyes which glowed a blood red by reflected light, they were known in other countries as "Siamese" cats. Here, in cold Tibet, they were *all* black. In the tropics, I was told, they were all white.

We wandered around, paying our respects to the Golden Images. Outside, the storm roared and fumed, blowing away all objects which were unsecured and making hazardous the passage of unwary travelers forced by urgent business to be upon the wind-swept roads. Here, though, in the Temple, all was quiet save for the muted "shush-shush" of many feet as pilgrims did their circuits, and the incessant "clack-chack" of the ever-turning Prayer Wheels. But we did not hear them. Day after day, night after night, the Wheels went round and round with their "clack-chack, clack-chack, clack-chack" until they had become a part of our existence; we heard them no more than we heard our heart-beats or our breath.

But there *was* another sound; a harsh, rasping *purr-purr* and the chink of the metal curtain as an old Tom butted his head against it to remind me that he and I were old friends. Idly I pushed my fingers through the links and scratched his head. Gently he "bit" my fingers in greeting, and then with his rough old tongue nearly scraped the skin off with the fervour of his licking! A suspicious movement further down the Temple—and he was off like a flash in order to protect "his" property.

"Wish we'd looked at the Shops!" whispered Timon. "Stupid!" whispered Yulgye, "you *know* they are shut during the storms." "Be quiet you boys!" said a fierce Proctor, stepping out of the shadows and aiming a blow which caught poor Timon off balance, and sent him sprawling to the floor. A nearby monk looked disapprovingly at the scene, and twirled his Prayer Wheel furiously. The great Proctor, almost seven feet tall, stood over us like a human mountain and hissed, "If you boys make another *squeak* . . . I'll tear you apart with my hands and toss the pieces to the dogs outside. Now, be *quiet*" With a last scowl in our direction, he turned and vanished into the shadows. Carefully, afraid of even the rustle of his robes, Timon rose to his feet. We slipped off our sandals and tiptoed to the door. Outside the storm was still raging; from the mountain pinnacles pennants of dazzlingly white snow streamed out. From lower reaches, from the Potala and Chakpori, *black* streams of dust and stones flowed. Along the Sacred Way great columns of dust raced into the City. The wind howled and screeched as if even the devils had gone crazy and were playing a mad cacophony without sense or reason.

Holding on to each other, we crept southwards round the Jo Kang, seeking the shelter of an alcove at the back of the Council Hall. The torrent of turbulent air threatened to lift us from our feet and blow us over the wall into the Tsang Kung Nunnery. We shivered at the mere thought, and pressed on to shelter. Our objective attained, we leaned back, our breath coming in great sobs from the efforts we had made. "* * * * *," said Timon, "I wish I could put a spell on that * * * * * Proctor! Your Honourable Guide could do it, Lobsang. Perhaps you could persuade him to turn that * * * * * into a pig," he added hopefully. I shook my head, "I am sure he would not," I replied, "for the Lama Mingyar Dondup never does ill to man or beast. Still, it *would* be nice to have the Proctor turn into something else. He *was* a bully!"

The storm was abating. Less shrill was the keening of the wind around the eaves. Pebbles previously wind-borne dropped to the roads and clattered against roof tops. Nor did the dust penetrate our robes so much. Tibet is a high and exposed country. Winds piled up behind the mountain ranges and rushed in fury through the passes, frequently flinging travellers to their deaths in the ravines. Gusts of wind roared through lamasery corridors, sweeping them clean, blowing away dust and litter before emerging to scream through the valley and on to the open stretches beyond.

The clamour and the tumult died. The last of the storm clouds raced across the sky leaving the vast vault of Heaven purple and pure. The harsh glare of the sun beat upon us, dazzling us with its brilliance after the murk and gloom of the storm. With grating creaks doors were cautiously opened; heads appeared and the damage of the day assessed. Poor old Mrs. Raks, near whose house we stood, had her front windows blown in and her rear windows blown out. In Tibet windows are of thick oiled paper, oiled so that one may, at some strain to the sight, see out.

Glass is rare indeed in Lhasa, paper made from the plentiful willow and rushes is cheap. We set out for home —Chakpori—stopping whenever any item of interest attracted our gaze.

"Lobsang!" said Timon, "say, *the shops will be open now!* Come on, it won't take long!" So saying, he turned off to the right at a much faster pace. Yulgye and I followed with just the merest show of reluctance. Arrived at The Street of Shops we looked eagerly about us. What wonders there were! The all-pervading smell of tea, many types of incense from India and China. Jewellery, and things from far off Germany which were so strange to us as to have no meaning. Further along we came to a shop where sweets were sold, sticky things on sticks, cakes covered with white sugar or coloured icing. We looked and longed; as poor chelas we had no money and so could buy nothing, but to look was free.

Yulgye nudged my arm and whispered, "Lobsang, that big fellow, isn't that Tzu who used to look after you?" I turned and stared in the direction where he pointed. Yes! It was Tzu all right, Tzu who had taught me so much and had been so very harsh with me. Instinctively I stepped forward and smiled up at him. "Tzu!" I said, "I am——" He scowled at me and snarled, "Get away, you boys, don't pester an honest citizen about his Master's business. You can't beg from *me*." He turned abruptly and strode away.

I felt my eyes grow hot and feared that I was going to disgrace myself in front of my friends. No, I could not afford the luxury of tears, but *Tzu* had ignored me, pretended not to know me. Tzu, who had taught me from birth. I thought how he had tried to teach me to ride my pony Nakkim, how he had taught me to wrestle. Now he had repudiated me—spurned me. I hung my head and disconsolately scratched the dust with my foot. By me, my two companions stood silent, awkward, feeling as I felt, feeling that they too had been slighted. A sudden movement attracted my attention; an elderly bearded Indian, wearing a turban, walked slowly toward me. "Young sir!"

he said in his queerly accented Tibetan, "I saw all, but think not ill of that man. Some of us have forgotten our childhood. I have not. Come with me." He led the way to the shop at which we had so recently gazed. "Let these young men take their pick," he said to the shopkeeper. Shyly each of us took one of those gorgeous sticky things and bowed gratefully to the Indian. *"No! No!"* he exclaimed, "one is not enough, take another each." We did so, and he paid the smiling shopkeeper. "Sir!" I said fervently, "may the Blessing of Buddha be with you and protect you; may your joys be many!" He smiled benignly upon us, bowed slightly, and turned away to continue his business.

Slowly we made our way home, slowly eating our sweets in order to make them last as long as possible. We had almost forgotten what such things tasted like. These tasted better than most because they had been given with such good feeling. I reflected, as we walked along, that first my Father had ignored me upon the steps of the Potala, and now Tzu had ignored me. Yulgye broke the silence; "It's a funny world, Lobsang, now we are boys we are ignored and snubbed. When we are lamas the Blackheads will come running for our favour!" In Tibet, the laity are referred to as "Blackheads" because they have hair on their heads; monks, of course, have shaven heads.

That evening at the Service I was very attentive; I determined to work hard so that I should become a lama as soon as possible, then I would stride among those "Blackheads" and spurn them when they sought my services. I was indeed so attentive that I attracted the attention of a Proctor. He regarded me with high suspicion, thinking such devotion from me was wholly unnatural! As soon as the Service ended I hurried away to my quarters as I knew I would have a busy day with the Lama Mingyar Dondup on the morrow. For some time I could not sleep. I tossed and turned and thought of the past and of the hardships I had undergone.

In the morning I arose and had my breakast and then

was about to make my way to the Lamas' Quarters. As I was leaving the room a hulking monk in a tattered robe grabbed me. "Hey, you!" he said, "*you* work in the kitchen this morning—cleaning millstones too!" "But Sir!" I replied, "my Guide the Lama Mingyar Dondup wants me." I attempted to squeeze past. "No, you come with me. Doesn't matter *who* wants you, I say you are going to work in the kitchen." He grabbed my arm and twisted it so that I could not escape. Reluctantly I went with him, there was no choice.

In Tibet we all took our turn at manual, at *menial* tasks. "Teaches humility!" said one. "Prevents a boy from getting above himself!" said another. "Knocks out class distinctions!" said a third. Boys—and monks—work at any task assigned purely as discipline. Of course, there was a domestic staff of lower-grade monks, but boys and monks of *all* grades had to take turns at the lowest and most unpleasant tasks as training. We all hated it as the "regulars"—inferior men all—treated us as slaves, well knowing that we could not possibly complain. Complain? It was *meant* to be hard!

Down the stone corridor we went. Down the steps made of two wooden uprights with bars fixed across. Into the great kitchens where I had been so badly burned on the leg. "There!" said the monk who was holding me, "get up and clean out the grooves in the stones." Picking up a sharp metal spike, I climbed on to one of the great barley-grinding wheels and industriously dug into the crushed debris lodged in the grooves. This stone had been neglected, and now, instead of grinding, it had just spoiled the barley. My task was to "dress" the surface so that it was again sharp and clean. The monk stood by, idly picking his teeth.

"Hey!" yelled a voice from the entrance, "Tuesday Lobsang Rampa. Is Tuesday Lobsang Rampa here? The Honourable Lama Mingyar Dondup wants him immediately." Instinctively I stood up and jumped off the stone. "Here I am!" I called. The monk brought his balled fist down hard on the top of my head, knocking me to the ground. "I say you will stay here and do your work," he growled. "If anyone wants you, let him come in person." Catching me by the neck, he lifted me and flung me on to the stone. My head struck a corner, and all the stars in the heavens flamed into my consciousness before fading and leaving the world blank and dark.

Strangely, I had a sensation of being lifted—lifted horizontally—and then stood on my feet. Somewhere a great, deep-toned gong seemed to be tolling out the seconds of life, it went "bong-bong-bong" and with a final stroke I felt that I had been struck by blue lightning. On the instant the world grew very bright, bright with a kind of yellowish light, a light in which I could see more clearly than normal. "Oooo," I said to myself, "so I am outside of my body! Oh! I do look strange!"

I had had considerable experience of astral travelling, I had travelled far beyond the confines of this old earth of ours, and I had travelled also to many of the greatest cities upon this globe. Now, though, I had my first experience of being "jumped out of my body." I stood beside the great mill-stone looking down with considerable distaste at the scruffy little figure in the very tattered robe lying on the stone. I gazed down, and it was only a matter of passing interest to observe how my astral body was joined to that battered figure by a bluish white cord which undulated and pulsed, which glowed brightly and faded, and glowed and faded again. Then I gazed more closely at my body upon this stone slab, and was appalled at the great gash over the left temple from whence oozed dark red blood, blood which seeped down into the stone grooves and mixed inextricably with the debris which so far had not been dug out.

A sudden commotion attracted my attention, and as I turned I saw my Guide, the Lama Mingyar Dondup, entering the kitchen, his face white with anger. He strode forward and came to a halt right before the head monk of the kitchen—the monk who had treated me so badly. No word was spoken, no word at all, in fact there was a hushed and deathly silence. My Guide's piercing eyes seemed to strike lightning into the kitchen monk, with a sigh like a punctured balloon he subsided into an inert mass on the stone floor. Without sparing a second glance at him my Guide turned away, turned to my earthly figure stretched out, breathing stertorously upon that stone circle.

I looked about me, I was really fascinated to think that I was now able to get out of my body for short distances. Going "far travels" in the astral was nothing, I always had been able to do that, but this sensation of getting out of myself and looking down upon my earthly suit of clay was a new, intriguing experience.

Ignoring the happenings about me for a moment, I let myself drift—drift up through the ceiling of the kitchen. "Ow!" I said involuntarily as I passed through the stone ceiling into the room above. Here were seated a group of lamas in deep contemplation. I saw with some interest that they had a sort of model of the world before them, it was a round ball upon which were indicated continents and lands and oceans and seas, and the round ball was fixed at an angle, the angle corresponding to the tilt of the earth itself in space. I did not tarry there, this seemed to me to be too much like lesson work, I journeyed upwards. Through another ceiling, through another, and yet another, and then I stood in the Room of the Tombs! About me were the great golden walls which supported the tombs of the Incarnations of the Dalai Lama for centuries past. I stood here in reverent contemplation for some moments, and then allowed myself to drift upwards, upwards, so that at last below me I saw that glorious Potala with all its gleaming gold, with all its scarlet and crimson and with the wondrous white walls which seemed to melt into the living rock of the mountain itself.

Turning my gaze slightly to the right I could see the Village of Shö and beyond that the City of Lhasa with the blue mountains in the background. As I rose I could see the limitless spaces of our fair and pleasant land, a land which could be hard and cruel through the vagaries of unpredictable weather but which, to me, was *home*!

A remarkably severe tugging attracted my attention and I found myself being reeled in as I often reeled in a kite which was soaring in the sky. I sank down and down, down into the Potala, through floors which became ceilings, and through floors again, until at last I reached my destination and stood again beside my body in the kitchen.

The Lama Mingyar Dondup was gently bathing my left temple—picking pieces from it. "Good gracious!" I said to myself in profound astonishment, "is my head so thick that it cracked or chipped the stone?" Then I saw that I had a small fracture, I saw also that a lot of the material being pulled from my head was debris—rubbish—the chippings of stone and the remnants of ground barley. I watched with interest, and—I confess—some amusement, for here standing beside my body in my astral body I felt no pain, no discomfort, only peace.

At last the Lama Mingyar Dondup finished his ministrations, and he put a patch, a herbal compress, upon my head and bound it about with silken bonds. Then, motioning to two monks who stood by with a litter, he instructed them to lift me so carefully.

The men—monks of my own Order—gently lifted me and placed me upon that litter, with the Lama Mingyar Dondup walking beside. I was carried off.

I looked about me in considerable astonishment, the light was fading, had I been so long that the day was dying? Before I had an answer to that I found that I too was fading, the yellow and the blue of the spiritual light was diminishing in intensity, and I felt an absolutely overwhelming, absolutely overpowering urge to rest—to sleep and not to bother about anything.

I knew no more for a time and then, through my head shot excruciating pains, pains which caused me to see reds and blues and greens and yellows, pains which made me think that I should go mad with the intense agony. A cool hand was placed upon me and a gentle voice said, "It is all right, Lobsang. It is all right, rest, rest, go to sleep!" The world seemed to become a dark fluffy pillow, the pillow was soft as swansdown into which I sank gratefully, peacefully, and the pillow seemed to envelop me so that I knew no more, and again my soul soared in space, while upon the earth my battered body remained at rest.

It must have been many hours later when I again regained consciousness, I awakened to find my Guide sitting beside me, holding my hands in his. As my eyelids fluttered upwards and the light of the evening streamed in, I smiled weakly, and he smiled back at me then, disengaging his hands, he took from a little table beside him a cup with some sweet smelling brew. Gently pressing it to my lips he said, "Drink this up, it will do you good!" I drank, and life flooded through me once again, so much so that I tried to sit up. The effort was too much; I felt as if a great club had been bashed down once more upon my head, I saw vivid lights, constellations of lights, and I soon desisted in my efforts.

The evening shadows lengthened, from below me came the muted sound of the conches, and I knew that the Service was about to start. My Guide, the Lama Mingyar Dondup, said, "I have to go for half an hour, Lobsang, because the Inmost One wants me, but your friends Timon and Yulgye are here to look after you in my absence and to call me should the occasion arise." He squeezed my hands, rose to his feet, and left the room.

Two familiar faces appeared, half frightened and wholly excited. They squatted down beside me, and Timon said, "Oh, Lobsang! Did the Kitchen Master get a telling off about all this!" "Yes," said the other, "and he is being turned out of the Lamasery for extreme, unnecessary brutality. He is being escorted out now!" They were bubbling with excitement, and then Timon said again, "I thought you were dead, Lobsang, you really did bleed like a stuffed yak!" I really had to smile as I looked at them, their voices showed how thrilled they were at any excitement to relieve the drab monotony of life in a lamasery. I held no grudge against them for their excitement, knowing that I too would have been excited if the victim had been other than I. I smiled upon them and was then overpowered by an oppressive tiredness. I closed my eyes, intending to rest them for a few moments, and once again I knew no more.

For several days, perhaps seven or eight in all, I rested upon my back and my Guide, the Lama Mingyar Dondup, acted as my nurse, but for him I should not have survived, for life in a lamasery is not necessarily gentle or kind, it is indeed survival of the fittest. The Lama was a kind man, a loving man, but even had he been otherwise there would have been the greatest reasons for keeping me alive. I, as I have said before, had a special task to do in life, and I supposed that the hardships which I was undergoing as a boy were meant in some way to toughen me, to make me become immured to hardship and suffering, for all the prophecies that I had heard—and I had heard quite a few! —had indicated that my life would be a life of sorrow, a life of suffering.

But it was not all suffering, as my condition improved there were more opportunities for talk with my Guide. We talked of many things, we covered common subjects and we covered subjects which were most uncommon. We dealt at length with various occult subjects. I remember on one occasion saying, "It must be a wonderful thing, Honourable Lama, to be a librarian and so possess all the knowledge in the world. I would be a librarian were it not for all these terrible prophecies as to my future." My Guide smiled down upon me. "The Chinese have a saying, 'a picture is worth a thousand words,' Lobsang, but I say that no amount of reading nor looking at pictures will replace practical experience and knowledge." I looked at him to see if he were serious and then I thought of the Japanese monk, Kenji Tekeuchi, who for almost seventy years had studied the printed word and had failed to practice or to absorb anything that he had read.

My Guide read my thoughts, "Yes!" he said, "the old man is not mental. He gave himself mental indigestion by

133

reading everything and anything and not absorbing any of it. He imagines that he is a great man, a man of surpassing spirituality. Instead he is a poor old blunderer who deceives no one so much as himself." The Lama sighed sadly and said, "He is spiritually bankrupt, knowing all but knowing nothing. The insensate, indiscriminate and ill-advised reading of all that comes one's way is dangerous. This man followed all the great religions and, understanding none of them, he yet set himself up as the greatest spiritual man of all."

"Honourable Lama!" I said, "if it be so harmful to have books, why are there books?" My Guide looked blankly at me for a moment. (*"Ha!"* I thought, "he does not know the answer to *that* one!") Then he smiled again and said, "But my dear Lobsang, the answer is so obvious! Read, read, and read again, but never let *any* book overpower your discrimination or your discernment. A book is meant to teach, to instruct or even to amuse. A book is *not* a master to be followed blindly and without reason. No person possessed of intelligence should ever be enslaved by a book or by the words of another." I sat back and nodded my head. Yes, that made sense. But then, *why bother with books*?

"Books, Lobsang?" said my Guide in answer to my query. "Of course there must be books! The libraries of the world contain most of the knowledge of the world, but no one but an idiot would say that mankind is the slave of books. Books exist merely to be a guide unto mankind, to be there for his reference, for his use. It is indeed a fact that books misused can be a curse, for they lead a man to feel that he is greater than he is and thus lead him to devious paths in life, paths which he has not the knowledge nor the wit to follow to the end." "Well, Honourable Lama," I asked again, "what are the uses of books?" My Guide looked hard at me and said, "You cannot go to all the places in the world and study under the greatest Masters of the world, but the printed word—books—can bring their teachings to you. You do not have to believe everything you read, nor do the great masters of writing ever tell you that you should, you should use your own judgment and use their words of wisdom as a pointer to what should be your words of wisdom. I can assure you that a person who is not ready to study a subject can harm himself immeasurably by getting hold of a book and—as it were—trying to raise himself above his karmic station by studying the words and the works of others. It may well be that the reader is a man of low evolutionary development, and in that case, in studying the things which at the present are not for him, he may stunt rather than enhance his spiritual development. I have known many such cases and our Japanese friend is just one."

My Guide rang for tea, a most necessary adjunct to all our discussions! When tea had been brought by the monk-servant we again resumed our discussion, My Guide said, "Lobsang! You are going to have a most unusual life, and to that end your development is being forced, your telepathic powers are being increased by any method at our disposal. I am going to tell you now that in just a few months you are going to study by telepathy allied to clairvoyance some of the greatest books of the world—some of the literary masterpieces of the world, and you are going to study them irrespective of lack of knowledge of the language in which they are written." I am afraid that I gaped at him in real astonishment, how could I study a book written in a language which I did not know? That was a matter which puzzled me, but I soon received an answer. "When your powers of telepathy and clairvoyance are a little more acute—as they will be—you will be able to pick up the whole thoughts of a book from people who have just recently read the book or are at present engaged upon such reading. This is one of the lesser known uses of telepathy which, of course, must in such cases be allied to clairvoyance. People in other parts of the world cannot always get to a public library or to one of the leading library centres of a country, they may pass the door but unless they can prove that they are a genuine student in search of knowledge, they are not admitted. Such a bar will not be placed on you, you will be able to travel in the astral and study and that will help you all the days of your life, and to the time when you pass beyond this life."

He told me of the uses of occultism. Misuse of occult power or the domination of another person by occult means brought a truly terrible punishment. Esoteric powers, metaphysical powers, and extrasensory perceptions were to be used only for good, only in the service of others, only to increase the sum total of knowledge contained in the world. "But, Honourable Lama!" I said, urgently, "how about people who get out of their bodies with excitement or with interest, how about when they fall out of their bodies and then nearly die of fright, can nothing be done to warn them?" My Guide smiled rather sadly at this as he said, "It is true, Lobsang, that many many people read books and try experiments without having a suitable Master at hand. Many people get out of themselves, either through drink or through over-excitement or through over-indulgence in something which is not good for the spirit, and then they panic. There is one way in which you can help, throughout your life you should warn those who enquire that the only thing to fear in occult matters is fear. Fear allows undesirable thoughts, undesirable entities to enter and even to take control of one, to take possession of one, and you, Lobsang, should repeat again and again that there is naught ever to fear other than fear itself. In casting out fear, then you strengthen humanity and make humanity purer. It is fear which causes wars, fear which makes dissension in the world, fear which turns man's hand against man. Fear, and fear alone, is the enemy, and if we throw out fear once and for all then—believe me—there is nothing more that need be feared."

Fear, what was all this talk about fear? I looked up at my Guide, and I suppose he saw the unspoken question in my eyes. Perhaps instead he read my thoughts telepathically, whatever it was he suddenly said, "So you are wondering about fear? Well, you are young and innocent!" I thought to myself, "Oh! Not so innocent as *he* thinks!" The Lama smiled as if he enjoyed that private joke with me—although of course I had not uttered a word—and then he said, "Fear is a very real thing, a tangible thing, you will have heard tales of those who are addicted to spirits—who become intoxicated. They are men who see remarkable creatures. Some of these drunkards claim to see green elephants with pink stripes, or even more bizarre creatures. I tell you, Lobsang, that the creatures which they see—so-called figments of their imagination—are real creatures indeed."

I was still not clear about this matter of fear. Of course I knew what fear was in the physical sense, I thought of the time when I had had to stay motionless outside the Chakpori Lamasery so that I could undergo the test of endurance before being permitted to enter and be accepted as the humblest of humble chelas. I turned to my Guide and said, "Honourable Lama, what *is* all this fear? In conversation I have heard of the creatures of the lower astral, yet I myself in all my astral travels have never encountered aught which caused me even a moment's fear. What *is* all this fear?"

My Guide sat still for a moment, then, as if reaching a sudden decision, he rose swiftly to his feet and said, "Come!" I rose also and we went along a stone corridor and turned to the right and to the left and to the right again. Continuing our journey we at last turned into a room where there was no light. It was like stepping into a pool of blackness, my Guide went first and lit a butter lamp which was standing ready beside the door, then, motioning to me to lie down, he said, "You are old enough to experience the entities of the lower astral. I am prepared to assist you to see these creatures and to make sure that you come to no harm, for they should not be encountered unless one is adequately prepared and protected. I will extinguish this light, and do you rest in peace and let yourself drift away from your body—let yourself drift whither you will, regardless of destination, regardless of intention—just drift and wander as the breeze." So saying he extinguished the lamp and there was no glimmer of light in that place when he had shut the door. I could not even detect his breathing but I could feel his warm, comforting presence near me.

Astral travelling was no new experience to me, I was born with the ability to travel thus and to remember always, everything. Now, stretched upon the ground, with my head resting upon part of my rolled-up robe, I folded my hands and put my feet together and dwelt upon the process of leaving the body, the process which is so simple to those who know. Soon I felt the gentle jerk which indicates a separation of the astral vehicle from the physical, and with that jerk there came a flooding of light. I seemed to be floating at the end of my Silver Cord. Beneath me was utter blackness, the blackness of the room which I had just left, and in which there was no glimmer of light. I looked about me, but this was in no way different from the normal travels that I had undertaken before. I thought of elevating myself above the Iron Mountain, and with the thought I was no longer in that room but hovering above the Mountain, hovering two perhaps three hundred feet. Suddenly I was no longer aware of the Potala, no longer aware of the Iron Mountain, no longer aware of the land of Tibet nor of the Valley of Lhasa. I felt sick with apprehension, my Silver Cord trembled violently and I was appalled to see that some of the "silver-blue" haze which always emanated from the Cord had turned into a sickly yellow-green.

Without warning there was a terrible twitching, a terrible tugging, a sensation as if insane fiends were trying to reel me in. Instinctively I looked down and nearly fainted away at what I saw.

About me, rather, below me, were the strangest and most hideous creatures such as were seen by drunks. The most horrible thing I had ever seen in my life came undulating toward me, it looked like an immense slug with an ugly human face but of such colours as no human ever wore. The face was red but the nose and ears were green, and the eyes seemed to revolve within their sockets. There were other creatures too, each seemed to be more horrible and more nauseating than the one before. I saw creatures which no words could describe yet they all seemed to have a common human trait of cruelty about them. They reached, they tried to pluck at me—they tried to tear me away from my Cord. Others reached down and tried to separate the Cord by pulling at it. I looked, and shuddered, and then I thought, "Fear! So *this* is fear! Well, these things cannot hurt me, I am immune from their manifestations, I am immune from their attacks!" And as I thought thus, the entities disappeared and were no more. The ethereal Cord joining me to my physical body brightened and reverted to its normal colours; I felt exhilarated, free, and I knew that in undergoing and surmounting this test I should not again be afraid of anything which could happen in the astral. It taught me conclusively that the things of which we are afraid cannot hurt us unless we permit them to hurt us through our fear.

A sudden tugging at my Silver Cord attracted my attention again and I looked down without the slightest hesitation, without the slightest sensation or feeling of fear. I saw a little glimmer of light, I saw that my Guide, the Lama Mingyar Dondup, had lighted that little flickering butter lamp, and my body was drawing down my astral body. Gently I floated down through the roof of the Chakpori, floated down so that I was horizontal above my physical body, then, gently so very gently, I drifted down and the astral and the physical merged and were as one. The body which was now "I" twitched slightly, and I sat up. My Guide looked down at me with a loving smile upon his face. "Well done, Lobsang!" he said. "To let you in to a very, very great secret, you did better on your first attempt than I did on mine. I am proud of you!"

I was still quite puzzled about this fear business, so I said, "Honourable Lama, what is there to be afraid of

139

really?" My Guide looked quite serious—even sombre—as he said, "You have led a good life, Lobsang, and have nothing to fear, therefore you do not fear. But there are those who have committed crimes, who have done wrongs against others, and when they are alone their consciences trouble them sorely. The creatures of the lower astral feed on fear, they are nourished by those of troubled conscience. People make thought forms of evil. Perhaps at some time in the future you will be able to go into an old, old cathedral or temple that has stood for countless years. From the walls of that building (such as our own Jo Kang) you will sense the good that has occurred within that building. But then if you can suddenly go to an old prison where much suffering, much persecution has taken place then you will have indeed the opposite effect. It follows from this that the inhabitants of buildings make thought forms which inhabit the walls of the buildings, wherefore it is apparent that a good building has good thought forms which give out good emanations, and places of evil have evil thoughts within them, wherefore it is again clear that only evil thoughts can come from an evil building, and those thoughts and thought forms can be seen and touched by those who are clairvoyant while in the astral state."

My Guide thought for a moment, and then said, "There are cases, as you will be aware, when monks and others imagine that they are greater than their own reality, they build a thought form and in time the thought form colours their whole outlook. There is a case which I recall at this moment of an old Burmese monk—a remarkably ignorant man too, I have to say—he was a lowly monk, a monk of no understanding, yet because he was our brother, and of our Order, we had to make every allowance. This monk lived a solitary life as do so many of us, but instead of devoting his time to meditation and contemplation and other things of good, he imagined instead that he was a mighty man in the land of Burma. He imagined that he was not a lowly monk who had hardly set foot upon the path of Enlightenment. Instead, in the solitude of his cell, he imagined that he was a great Prince, a Prince of mighty estates and great wealth. At the start it was harmless, it was a harmless if useless diversion. Certainly no one would have condemned him for a few idle imaginings and yearnings, for, as I say, he had neither the wit nor the learning to really devote himself to the spiritual tasks at hand. This man throughout the years, whenever he was alone, became the great, great Prince. It coloured his outlook, it affected his manner, and with the passage of time the humble monk seemed to disappear and the arrogant Prince came to the fore. At last the poor unfortunate man really believed most firmly that he was a Prince of the land of Burma. He spoke to an Abbot one day as if the Abbot was a serf upon the princely estate. The Abbot was not such a peaceful Abbot as some of us, and I am sorry to say that the shock which the poor monk-turned-princeling sustained put him off balance, and reduced him to a state of mental instability. But you, Lobsang, have no need to worry about such things; you are stable and well balanced and without fear. Remember only these words by way of warning: Fear corrodes the soul. Vain and useless imaginings put one on the wrong path so that with the passage of years the imaginings become reality, and the realities fade from sight and do not come to light again for several incarnations. Keep your foot upon the Path, let no wild yearning nor imaginings colour or distort your outlook. This is the World of Illusion, but to those of us who can face that knowledge, then the illusion can be turned into reality when we are off this world."

I thought of all that, and I must confess that I had already heard of that monk-turned-mental-prince, because I had read about it in some book in the Lamas' Library. "Honourable Guide!" I said, "what are the uses of occult power, then?" The Lama folded his hands and looked straight at me. "The uses of occult knowledge? Well, that is easy enough, Lobsang! We are entitled to help those who are worthy of help. We are not entitled to help those

141

who do not want our help, and are not yet ready for help. We do not use occult power or ability for self-gain, nor for hire or reward. The whole purpose of occult power is to speed one's development upwards, to speed one's evolution and to help the world as a whole, not just the world of humans, but the world of nature, of animals—everything."

We were again interrupted by the Service starting in the Temple building near us, and as it would have been disrespectful to the Gods to continue a discussion while they were being worshipped, we ended our talk and sat in silence by the flickering flame of the butter lamp, now burning low.

CHAPTER EIGHT

It was pleasant indeed lying in the cool, long grass at the base of the Pargo Kaling. Above me, at my back, the ancient stones soared heavenwards and, from my viewpoint flat on the ground, the point so high above seemed to scrape the clouds. Appropriately enough, the "Bud of the Lotus" forming the point symbolised Spirit, while the "leaves" which supported the "Bud" represented Air. I, at the base, rested comfortably against the representation of "Life on Earth." Just beyond my reach—unless I stood—were the "Steps of Attainment." Well, I was trying to "attain" now!

It was pleasant lying here and watching the traders from India, China and Burma come trudging by. Some of them were afoot while leading long trains of animals carrying exotic goods from far, far places. Others, more grand maybe, or possibly just plain tired, rode and gazed about. I speculated idly on what their pannier bags contained, then pulled myself together with a jerk; *that was why I was here!* I was here to watch the aura of as many different people as I could. I was here to "divine" from the aura and from telepathy what these men were doing, what they were thinking, and what were their intentions.

Just off to the opposite side of the road a poor blind beggar sat. He was covered with dirt. Ragged and commonplace he sat and whined at passing travellers. A surprising number threw coins to him, delighting in watching him, blind, scrabble for the fallen coins and finally locate them by the sound they made as they struck the earth and perhaps chinked against a stone. Occasionally, very occasionally indeed, he would miss a small coin, and the

143

traveller would lift it and drop it again. Thinking of him, I turned my lazy head in his direction and sat upright in sheer dazed astonishment. His aura! I had never bothered to observe it before. Now, looking carefully, I saw that he was not blind, I saw that he was rich, had money and goods stored away and that he was pretending to be a poor blind beggar as it was the easiest way of making a living that he knew. No! It could not be, I was mistaken, I was overconfident or something. Perhaps my powers were failing. Troubled at such a thought, I stumbled to my reluctant feet and went in search of enlightenment from my Guide the Lama Mingyar Dondup who was at the Kundu Ling opposite.

Some weeks before I had undergone an operation in order that my "Third Eye" might be the more widely opened. From birth I had been possessed of unusual powers of clairvoyance, with the ability to see the "aura" around the bodies of humans, animals and plants. The painful operation had succeeded in increasing my powers far more than had been anticipated even by the Lama Mingyar Dondup. Now my development was being rushed; my training in all occult matters occupied my waking hours. I felt squeezed by mighty forces as *this* lama and *that* lama "pumped" knowledge into me by telepathy and by other strange forces whose workings I was now so intensively studying. Why do classwork when one can be taught by telepathy? Why wonder at a man's intentions when one can see from his aura? But I was wondering about that blind man!

"Ow! Honourable Lama! Where are you?" I cried, running across the road in search of my Guide. Into the little park I stumbled, almost tripping over my own eager feet. "So!" smiled my Guide, sitting peacefully on a fallen bole, "So! You are excited, you have just discovered that the 'blind' man sees as well as you." I stood panting, panting from lack of breath and from indignation. "Yes!" I exclaimed, "the man is a fraud, a robber, for he steals from those of good heart. He should be put in prison!"

144

The Lama burst out laughing at my red, indignant face. "But Lobsang," he said mildly, "why all the commotion? That man is selling service as much as the man who sells prayer-wheels. People give insignificant coins to him that they may be thought generous; it makes them feel good. For a time it increases their rate of molecular vibration— raises their spirituality—places them nearer the Gods. It does them good. The coins they give? Nothing! They do not miss them." "But he is not blind!" I said in exasperation, "he is a *robber*." "Lobsang," said my Guide, "he is harmless, he is selling service. Later, in the Western World, you will find that advertising people will make claims the falsity of which will injure one's health, will deform babies yet unborn, and will transform the passably sane into raving maniacs."

He patted the fallen tree and motioned for me to sit beside him. I sat and drummed my heels on the bark. "You must practice using the aura and telepathy together," said my Guide. "By using one and not the other your conclusions may be warped—as in this case. It is essential to use all one's faculties, bring all one's powers to bear, on each and every problem. Now, this afternoon I have to go away, and the great Medical Lama, the Reverend Chinrobnobo, of the Menzekang Hospital, will talk to you. And you will talk to him." "Ow!" I said, ruefully, "but he never speaks to me, never even notices me!" "All that will be changed—one way or another—this afternoon," said my Guide. "One way or another!" I thought. That looked very ominous.

Together my Guide and I walked back to the Iron Mountain, pausing momentarily to gaze anew at the old yet always fresh coloured rock carvings. Then we ascended the steep and stony path. "Like life, this path, Lobsang," said the Lama. "Life follows a hard and stony path, with many traps and pitfalls, yet if one perseveres the top is attained." As we reached the top of the path the call to Temple Service was made, and we each went our own way, he to his associates, and I to others of my class. As soon

145

as the Service had ended, and I had partaken of food, a chela even smaller than I came somewhat nervously to me. "Tuesday Lobsang," he said diffidently, "the Holy Medical Lama Chinrobnobo wants to see you immediately in the Medical School."

I straightened my robe, took a few deep breaths that my twanging nerves might be calmed, and walked with assurance that I did not feel over to the Medical School. "Ah!" boomed a great voice, a voice that reminded me of the sound of a deep Temple conch. I stood before him and paid my respects in the time-honoured way. The Lama was a big man, tall, bulky, broad-shouldered, and a wholly awe-inspiring figure for a small boy. I felt that a swipe from one of his mighty hands would knock my head straight off my shoulders and send it tumbling down the mountainside. However, he bade me be seated before him, bade me in such a genial manner that I almost fell into a sitting position!

"Now, boy!" said the great deep voice, like rolling thunder among the distant mountains. "I have heard much of you. Your Illustrious Guide, the Lama Mingyar Dondup claims that you are a prodigy, that your para-normal abilities are immense. We shall see!" I sat and quaked. "You see me? What do you see?" he asked. I quaked even more as I said the first thing that entered my mind; "I see such a big man, Holy Medical Lama, that I thought it was a mountain when I came here first." His boisterous laugh caused such a gale of wind that I half feared that it would blow my robe off. "Look at me, boy, *look at my aura* and tell me what you see!" he commanded. Then, "Tell me what you see of the aura and what it means to you." I looked at him, not directly, not staring, for that often dims the aura of a clothed figure; I looked toward him, but not exactly "at" him.

"Sir!" I said, "I see first the physical outline of your body, dimly as it would be without a robe. Then, very close to you I see a faint bluish light the colour of fresh wood smoke. It tells me that you have been working too

146

hard, that you have had sleepless nights of late and your etheric energy is low." He looked at me with eyes somewhat wider than normal, and nodded in satisfaction. "Go on!" he said.

"Sir!" I continued, "your aura extends from you a distance of about nine feet on either side. The colours are in layers both vertical and horizontal. You have the yellow of high spirituality. At present you are marvelling that one of my age can tell you so much and you are thinking that my Guide the Lama Mingyar Dondup knows something after all. You are thinking that you will have to apologize to him for your expressed doubts as to my capabilities." I was interrupted by a great shout of laughter. "You are right, boy, you are right!" he said delightedly, *"Go on!"*

"Sir!" (this was child's play to me!) "You recently had some mishap and sustained a blow over your liver. It hurts when you laugh too hard and you wonder if you should take some tatura herb and have deep massage while under its anaesthetic influence. You are thinking that it is Fate which decided that of more than six thousand herbs, tatura should be in short supply." He was not laughing now, he was looking at me with undisguised respect. I added, "It is further indicated in your aura, Sir, that in a short time you will be the most important Medical Abbot of Tibet."

He gazed at me with some apprehension. "My boy," he said, "you have great power—you will go far. Never *never* abuse the power within you. It can be dangerous. Now let us discuss the aura as equals. But let us discuss over tea." He raised the small silver bell and shook it so violently that I feared it would fly from his hand. Within seconds a young monk hastened in with tea and—oh, joy of joys!— some of the luxuries of Mother India! As we sat there I reflected that all these high lamas had comfortable quarters. Below us I could see the great parks of Lhasa, the Dodpal and the Khati were—so it appeared—within reach of my extended arm. More to the left the Chorten of our area, the Kesar Lhakhang, stood like a sentinel, while across the road, further north, my favourite spot, the Pargo Kaling (Western Gate) towered aloft.

"What causes the aura, Sir?" I asked. "As your respected Guide, the Lama Mingyar Dondup has told you," he commenced, "the brain receives messages from the Overself. Electric currents are generated in the brain. The whole of Life is electric. The aura is a manifestation of electric power. About one's head, as you so well know, there is a halo or nimbus. Old paintings always show a Saint or God with such a 'Golden Bowl' around the back of the head." "Why do so few people see the aura and the halo, Sir?" I asked. "Some people disbelieve the existence of the aura because *they* can not see it. They forget that they can not see air either, and without air they would not manage very well! Some—a very, very few—people see auras. Others do not. Some people can hear higher frequencies, or lower frequencies than others. It has nothing to do with the degree of spirituality of the observer, any more than the ability to walk on stilts indicates a necessarily spiritual person." He smiled at me and added, "I used to walk on stilts almost as well as you. Now my figure is not suited for it." I smiled too, thinking that he would need a pair of tree trunks as stilts.

"When we operated upon you for the Opening of the Third Eye," said the Great Medical Lama, "we were able to observe that portions of your frontal-lobe developments were very different from the average and so we assume that physically you were *born* to be clairvoyant and telepathic. That is one of the reasons you have received and *will* receive such intensive and advanced training." He looked at me with immense satisfaction and continued, "You are going to have to remain here at the Medical School for a few days. We are going to investigate you thoroughly and see how we can even increase your abilities and teach you much." There was a discreet cough at the door, and my Guide the Lama Mingyar Dondup walked into the room. I jumped to my feet and bowed to him—as did the Great Chinrobnobo. My Guide was smiling. "I received your telepathic message," he said to the Great Medical Lama, "so I came to you as speedily as I was able so that perhaps you would give me the pleasure of hearing your confirmation of my findings in the case of my young friend." He stopped, and smiled at me and sat down.

The Great Lama Chinrobnobo also smiled and said, "Respected Colleague! I gladly bow to your superior knowledge in accepting this young man for investigation. Respected Colleague, your own talents are numerous, you are startlingly versatile, but never have you found such a boy as this." Then, of all things, they both laughed, and the Lama Chinrobnobo reached down somewhere behind him and took out—three jars of pickled walnuts! I must have looked stupid for they both turned toward me and started laughing. "Lobsang, you are not using your telepathic ability. If you were you would be aware that the Reverend Lama and I were so sinful as to have a bet. It was agreed between us that if you came up to my statements, then the Reverend Medical Lama would give you three jars of pickled walnuts, whereas if you were not up to the standard claimed by me I would do a long journey and undertake certain medical work for my friend."

My Guide smiled at me again and said, "Of course I am going to do the journey for him in any case, and you will be going with me, but we had to get matters straight and now honour is satisfied." He pointed to the three jars and said, "Put them by you, Lobsang, when you leave here— when you leave this room—take them with you for they are the spoils of the victor, and in this case you are the victor." I really felt remarkably foolish, obviously I could not use telepathic powers on these two High Lamas. The very thought of such a thing sent chill shivers along my spine. I loved my Guide the Lama Mingyar Dondup, and I greatly respected the knowledge and wisdom of the Great Lama Chinrobnobo. It would have been an insult, it would have been bad manners indeed to have eavesdropped even telepathically. The Lama Chinrobnobo turned to me

149

and said, "Yes, my boy, your sentiments do you credit. I am pleased indeed to greet you and to have you here among us. We will help you with your development."

My Guide said, "Now Lobsang, you are going to have to stay in this particular building for, perhaps a week, because you are going to be taught quite a lot about the aura. Oh yes!" he said, interpreting my glance, "I am aware that you think you know all about the aura. You can see the aura, and you can read the aura, but now you have to learn the whys and wherefores of it and you have to learn how much the other fellow does not see. I am going to leave you now, but I shall see you tomorrow." He rose to his feet and, of course, we rose as well. My Guide made his farewells and then withdrew from that quite comfortable chamber. The Lama Chinrobnobo turned to me and said, "Do not be so nervous, Lobsang, nothing is going to happen to you—we are merely going to try to help you and to expedite your own development. First of all, let us have a little discussion about the human aura. You of course see the aura vividly and you can understand about the aura, but imagine that you were not so favoured —not so gifted, put yourself in the position of ninety nine and nine tenths, or even more, of the world's population." He violently rang that little silver bell again and once again the attendant came bustling in with tea and of course the necessary "other things" which most pleased me when I was having tea! It might be of interest here to say that we in Tibet sometimes drank in excess of sixty cups of tea in a day. Of course, Tibet is a cold country and the hot tea warmed us, we were not able to get out and buy drinks such as people of the Western world had, we were limited to tea and tsampa unless some really kind-hearted person brought from a land such as India those things which were not available in Tibet.

We settled down, and the Lama Chinrobnobo said, "We have already discussed the origin of the aura. It is the life force of a human body. I am going to assume for the moment, Lobsang, that you cannot see the aura and that

150

you know nothing about the aura, because only in assuming that can I tell you what the average person sees and does not see." I nodded my head to indicate that I understood. Of course I had been born with the ability to see the aura and things like that, and those abilities had been increased by the operation of "the Third Eye," and on many occasions in the past I had been almost trapped into saying what I saw, without it dawning upon me that others did not see the same as I. I remembered an occasion sometime previously when I had said that a person was still alive—a person that old Tzu and I had seen lying beside the road—and Tzu had said that I was quite wrong, the man was dead. I had said, "But Tzu, the man still has his lights on!" Fortunately, as I realised after, the gale of wind which was blowing past us had distorted my words so that Tzu had not comprehended the meaning. On some impulse, however, he had examined the man lying beside the road and found he was alive! But this is a digression.

"The average man and woman, Lobsang, cannot see the human aura. Some, indeed, hold to the belief that there is no such thing as a human aura. They might just as well say that there is no such thing as air because they cannot see it!" The Medical Lama looked at me to see if I was following him or if my thoughts were straying walnut-wise. Satisfied with my appearance of attention, he nodded sagely and continued, "So long as there is life in a body, then there is an aura which can be seen by those with the power or gift or ability—call it what you will. I must explain to you, Lobsang, that for the clearest perception of the aura the subject who is being seen must be absolutely nude. We will discuss why later. It is sufficient for just ordinary readings to look at a person while they have some clothing on, but if you are going to look for anything whatever connected with a medical reason, then the person must be completely and absolutely nude. Well, completely enveloping the body and extending from the body for a distance of an eighth of an inch to three or four inches is the etheric sheath. This is a blue-grey mist,

151

one can hardly call it a mist, for although it appears misty one can see clearly through it. This etheric covering is the purely animal emanation, it derives particularly from the animal vitality of the body so that a very healthy person will have a quite wide etheric, it may even be three or four inches from the body. Only the most gifted, Lobsang, perceive the next layer, for between the etheric and the aura proper there is another band, perhaps three inches across, and one has to be gifted and talented indeed to see any colours in that band. I confess that I can see nothing but empty space there."

I felt really gleeful about that, because I could see all the colours in that space and I hastened to say so. "Yes, yes, Lobsang! I know you can see in that space, for you are one of our most talented in this direction, but I was pretending that you could not see the aura at all because I have to explain all this to you." The Medical Lama looked at me reprovingly—reprovingly, no doubt, for interrupting the trend of his thoughts. When he thought that I was sufficiently subdued to refrain from further interruption he continued, "First, then, there is the etheric layer. Following the etheric layer there is that zone which so few of us can distinguish except as an empty space. Outside of that is the aura itself. The aura does not so much depend upon the animal vitality as upon the spiritual vitality. The aura is composed of swirling bands, and striations of all the colours of the visible spectrum, and that means more colours than can be seen with the physical eyes, for the aura is seen by other senses than by the physical sight. Every organ in the human body sends out its own shaft of light, its shaft of rays, which alter and fluctuate as the thoughts of a person fluctuate. Many of these indications are present to a very marked degree in the etheric and in the space beyond, and when the nude body is seen the aura appears to magnify the indications of health or disease, from which it is clear that those of us who are sufficiently clairvoyant can tell of a person's health or otherwise."

I knew all about that, this was all child's play to me, and I had been practising things like this ever since the operation for "the Third Eye." I knew of the groups of Medical Lamas who sat beside suffering people and examined the nude body to see how they could be helped. I had thought perhaps that I was going to be trained for work such as that.

"Now!" said the Medical Lama, "you are being specially trained, highly trained, and when you go to that great Western world beyond our borders it is hoped and thought that you may be able to devise an instrument whereby even those with no occult power at all will be able to see the human aura. Doctors, seeing the human aura, and actually seeing what is wrong with a person, will be able to cure that person's illnesses. How, we shall discuss later. I know that all this is quite tiring, much of that which I have told you is very well known indeed to you, but it may be tiring from this aspect; you are a natural clairvoyant, you may possibly never have thought of the mechanics of the operation of your gift, and that is a matter which must be remedied because a man who knows only half a subject is only half trained and half useful. You, my friend, are going to be very useful indeed! But let us end this session now, Lobsang, we will repair to our own apartments—for one has been set aside for you—and then we can rest and think on those matters upon which we have so briefly touched. For this week you will not be required to attend any Service, that is by order of the Inmost One Himself, all your energies, all your devotions, are to be directed solely to mastering the subjects which I and my colleagues are going to put before you."

He rose to his feet and I rose to mine. Once again that silver bell was seized in a mighty hand and shaken so vigorously that I really felt that the poor thing would fall to pieces. The attendant monk came running in and the Medical Lama Chinrobnobo said, "You will attend upon Tuesday Lobsang Rampa, for he is an honoured guest here as you are aware. Treat him as you would treat a visiting monk of high degree." He turned to me and bowed, and of course I hastily bowed back, and then the attendant beckoned for me to follow him. "Stop!" bawled the Lama Chinrobnobo. "You have forgotten your walnuts!" I rushed back and hastily grabbed up those precious jars smiling somewhat in embarrassment as I did so, then I hastened on to the waiting attendant.

We went along a short corridor and the attendant ushered me into a very nice room which had a window overlooking the ferry across The Happy River. "I am to look after you, Master," said the attendant. "The bell is there for your convenience, use it as you will." He turned and went out. I turned to that window. The view across the Holy Valley entranced me, for the ferry of inflated yak hides was just putting out from the shore and the boatman was poling along across the swift river. On the other side, I saw, there were three or four men who, by their dress, must have been of some importance—an impression which was confirmed by the obsequious manner of the ferryman. I watched for some minutes, and then, suddenly, I felt more tired than I could imagine possible. I sat down upon the ground without even bothering about a seat cushion, and before I knew anything about it I had toppled over backwards, asleep.

The hours droned away to the accompaniment of clacking Prayer Wheels. Suddenly I sat up, bolt upright, quaking with fear. *The Service!* I was late for the Service. With my head on one side I listened carefully. Somewhere a voice was chanting a Litany. It was enough—I jumped to my feet and raced for the familiar door. It was not there! With a bone-jarring thud I collided with the stone wall and fell bouncily onto my back. For a moment, there was a blue-white flash inside my head as it too struck the stone, then I recovered and sprang to my feet once more. Panicked at my lateness, I raced around the room and there seemed to be no door. Worse—there was no window either!

"Lobsang!" said a voice from the darkness, "are you ill?" The voice of the attendant brought me back to my senses like a dash of iced water. "Oh!" I said sheepishly, "I forgot, I thought I was late for Service. I forgot I was excused!" There was a subdued chuckle, and the voice said, "I will light the lamp, for it is very dark this night." A little glimmer came from the doorway—it was in a *most* unexpected place!—and the attendant advanced towards me. "A most amusing interlude," he said, "I thought at first that a herd of yaks had broken loose and were in here." His smile robbed the words of all offence. I settled down again, and the attendant and his light withdrew. Across the lighter darkness that was the window a shooting star flamed into incandescence, and its journey across the countless miles of space was at an end. I rolled over and slept.

Breakfast was the same old dull and dreary tsampa and tea. Nourishing, sustaining, but uninspiring. Then the attendant came and said, "If you are ready, I have to take you elsewhere." I rose to my feet and walked with him out of the room. We went a different way this time, into a part of the Chakpori which I did not know existed. Downwards, a long way downwards until I thought we were descending into the bowels of the Iron Mountain itself. Now there was no glimmer of light except from the lamps we carried. At last the attendant stopped, and pointed ahead. "Go on—straight along and turn into the room on the left." With a nod, he turned and retraced his steps.

I trudged on, wondering, "What now?" The Room on the Left was before me, I turned into it and paused in amazement. The first thing to attract my attention was a Prayer Wheel standing in the middle of the room. I had time for only a brief glance at it, but even so it appeared to be a very strange Prayer Wheel indeed, then my name was spoken. "Well, Lobsang! We are glad you are here." I looked and there was my Guide, the Lama Mingyar Dondup, by his side sat the Great Medical Lama Chinrobnobo, and on the other side of my Guide there sat a very distinguished-looking Indian Lama named Marfata. He had once studied Western medicine, and had indeed

155

studied at some German University which I believe was called Heidelberg. Now he was a Buddhist monk, a lama, of course, but "monk" is the generic term.

The Indian looked at me so searchingly, so piercingly, that I thought he must be looking at the material comprising the back of my robe—he seemed to look right through me. However, on this particular occasion I had nothing bad on my conscience, and I returned his gaze. After all, why should I not gaze at him? I was as good as he, for I was being trained by the Lama Mingyar Dondup and by the Great Medical Lama Chinrobnobo. A smile forced its way across his rigid lips as if its execution caused him intense pain. He nodded, and turned to my Guide, "Yes, I am satisfied that the boy is as you say." My Guide smiled—but there was no forcing of his smile, it was natural, spontaneous, and indeed warming to the heart.

The Great Medical Lama said, "Lobsang, we have brought you down here to this secret room because we want to show you things and discuss things with you. Your Guide and I have examined you and we are indeed satisfied with your powers, powers that are going to be increased in intensity. Our Indian colleague, Marfata, did not think that such a prodigy existed in Tibet. We hope that you will prove all our statements." I looked at that Indian and I thought, "Well, he is a man who has an exalted opinion of himself." I turned to the Lama Chinrobnobo and said, "Respected Sir, the Inmost One who has been good enough to give me an audience on a number of occasions has expressly cautioned me against giving proof, saying that proof was merely a palliative to the idle mind. Those who wanted proof were not capable of accepting the truth of a proof no matter how well proven." The Medical Lama Chinrobnobo laughed so that I almost feared I would be blown away by the gale of wind; my Guide also laughed, and they both looked at the Indian Marfata who sat looking sourly at me. "Boy!" said the Indian, "you talk well, but talk proves nothing as you yourself say. Now, tell me, boy, what do you see in me?" I felt rather apprehensive about this, because much of what I saw I did not like. "Illustrious Sir!" I said, "I fear that if I say what I see then you might indeed take it amiss and consider that I am being merely insolent instead of replying to your question." My Guide the Lama Mingyar Dondup nodded in agreement, and across the face of the Great Medical Lama Chinrobnobo a huge, beaming smile expanded like the rising of the full moon. "Say what you will, boy, for we have no time for fancy talk here," said the Indian.

For some moments I stood looking at the Great Indian Lama, stood looking until even he stirred a little at the intensity of my gaze, then I said, "Illustrious Sir! You have commanded me to speak as I see, and I understand that my Guide the Lama Mingyar Dondup and the Great Medical Lama Chinrobnobo also want me to speak frankly. Now, this is what I see, I have never seen you before but from your aura and from your thoughts I detect this: You are a man who has travelled extensively, and you have travelled across the great oceans of the world. You have gone to that small island whose name I do not know, but where the people are all white and where there is another small island lying nearby as if it were a foal to the greater island which was the mare. You were very antagonistic toward those people and they were indeed anxious to take some action against you for something connected with—" I hesitated here, for the picture was particularly obscure, it was referring to things of which I had not the slightest knowledge. However, I ploughed on—"There was something connected with an Indian city which I assume from your mind was Calcutta, and there was something connected with a black hole where the people of that island were gravely inconvenienced or embarrassed. In some way they thought that you could have saved trouble instead of causing it." The Great Lama Chinrobnobo laughed again, and it did my ears good to hear that laugh because it indicated that I was on the right track. My Guide gave no indication whatever, but the Indian snorted.

I continued, "You went to another land and I can see the name Heidelberg clearly in your mind. In that land you studied medicine according to many barbarous rites wherein you did much cutting and chopping and sawing, and did not use systems which we here in Tibet use. Eventually you were given some sort of big paper with a lot of seals upon it. I see also from your aura that you are a man with an illness." I took a deep breath here because I did not know how my next words would be received. "The illness from which you suffer is one which has no cure, it is one in which the cells of the body run wild and grow as weeds grow, not according to pattern, not according to the ordained way, but spread and obstruct and clutch at vital organs. Sir! You are ending your own span upon this earth by the nature of your thoughts which admit of no goodness in the minds of others." For several moments—they may have been years to me!—there was not a sound, and then the Great Medical Lama Chinrobnobo said, "That is perfectly correct, Lobsang, that is perfectly correct!" The Indian said, "The boy was probably primed about all this in advance."

My Guide, the Lama Mingyar Dondup said, "No one has discussed you, on the contrary much of what he has told us is news to us, for we have not investigated your aura nor your mind for you did not so invite us. But the main point at issue is, the boy Tuesday Lobsang Rampa has these powers, and the powers are going to be developed even further. We have no time for quarrels, no place for quarrels, instead we have serious work to do. Come!" He rose to his feet and led me to that big Prayer Wheel.

I looked at that strange thing, and I saw that it was not a Prayer Wheel after all, but instead was a device standing about four feet high, four feet from the ground, and it was about five feet across. There were two little windows at one side and I could see what appeared to be glass set in those windows. At the other side of the machine, and set off-centre, were two very much larger windows. At an opposite side a long handle protruded, but the whole thing was a mystery to me, I had not the slightest idea of what it could be. The Great Medical Lama said, "This is a device, Lobsang, with which those who are not clairvoyant can see the human aura. The Great Indian Lama Marfata came here to consult us and would not tell us the nature of his complaint, saying that if we knew so much about esoteric medicine we would know his complaint without his telling us. We brought him here that he could be examined with this machine. With his permission he is going to remove his robe, and you are going to look at him first, and you are going to tell us just what his trouble is. Then we shall use this machine and see how far your finding and the findings of the machine coincide."

My Guide indicated a spot against a dark wall and the Indian walked to it and removed his robe and other garments so that he stood brown and bare against the wall. "Lobsang! Take a very good look at him and tell us what you see," said my Guide. I looked not at the Indian, but some way to one side, I put my eyes out of focus as that is the easiest way of seeing the aura. That is, I did not use normal binocular vision, but instead saw with each eye separately. It is a difficult thing indeed to explain, but it consisted in looking with one eye to the left and one eye to the right, and that is just a knack—a trick—which can be learned by almost anyone.

I looked at the Indian, and his aura glowed and fluctuated. I saw that he was a great man indeed and of high intellectual power but, unfortunately, his whole outlook had been soured by the mysterious illness within him. As I looked at him I spoke my thoughts, spoke them just as they came into my mind. I was not at all aware of how intently my Guide and the Great Medical Lama were listening to my words. "It is clear that the illness has been brought on by many tensions within the body. The Great Indian Lama has been dissatisfied and frustrated, and that has acted against his health, causing the cells of his body to run wild, to escape from the direction of the Overself. Thus he has this complaint here" (I pointed to his liver) "and because he is a rather sharp tempered man his complaint is aggravated every time he gets cross. It is clear from his aura that if he would become more tranquil, more placid, like my Guide the Lama Mingyar Dondup, he would stay upon this earth longer and so would accomplish more of his task without the necessity of having to come again."

Once again there was a silence, and I was pleased to see that the Indian Lama nodded as if in complete agreement with my diagnosis. The Medical Lama Chinrobnobo turned to that strange machine and looked through the little windows. My Guide moved to the handle and turned with increasing force until a word from the Medical Lama Chinrobnobo caused him to maintain the rate of rotation at a constant speed. For some time the Lama Chinrobnobo gazed through that device, then he straightened up and without a word the Lama Mingyar Dondup took his place, while the Medical Lama Chinrobnobo turned the handle as my Guide had previously. Eventually they finished their examination, and stood together obviously conversing by telepathy. I made no attempt whatever to intercept their thoughts, because to do so would have been a gross slight and would have put me "above my station." At last, they turned to the Indian and said, "All that Tuesday Lobsang Rampa has told you is correct. We have examined your aura most thoroughly, and we believe that you have cancer of the liver. We believe also that this has been caused by a certain shortness of temper. We believe that if you will lead a quiet life you still have a number of years left to you, years in which you can accomplish your task. We are prepared to make representations so that if you agree to our plan you will be permitted to remain here at Chakpori."

The Indian discussed matters for a time, and then motioned to Chinrobnobo, together they left the room. My Guide the Lama Mingyar Dondup patted me on the shoulder and said, "Well done, Lobsang, well done! Now I want to show this machine to you."

He walked across to that very strange device and lifted up one side of the top. The whole thing moved, and inside I saw a series of arms radiating from a central shaft. At the extreme end of the arms there were prisms of glass in ruby red, blue, yellow and white. As the handle was turned belts connected from it to the shaft caused the arms to rotate, and I observed that each prism in turn was brought into the line which was seen by looking through the two eyepieces. My Guide showed me how the thing worked and then said, "Of course this is a very crude and clumsy affair. We use it here for experiment, and in the hope of one day producing a smaller version. You would never need to use it, Lobsang, but there are not many who have the power of seeing the aura as clearly as you. At some time I shall explain the working in more detail, but briefly, it deals with a heterodyne principle wherein rapidly rotating coloured prisms interrupt the line of sight and thus destroy the normal image of the human body and intensify the much weaker rays of the aura." He replaced the lid and turned away to another device standing on a table at a far corner. He was just leading the way to that table when the Medical Lama Chinrobnobo came into the room again and joined us. "Ah!" he said, coming over to us, "so you are going to test his thought power? Good! I must be in on this!" My Guide pointed to a queer cylinder of what appeared to be rough paper. "This, Lobsang, is thick, rough paper. You will see that it has innumerable holes made in it, holes made with a very blunt instrument so that the paper is torn and leaves projections. We then folded that paper so that all the projections were on the outside and the sheet, instead of being flat, formed a cylinder. Across the top of the cylinder we affixed a rigid straw, and upon a small pedestal we fixed a sharp needle. Thus we have the cylinder supported on an almost frictionless bearing. Now watch me!" He sat down, and put his hands on either side of the cylinder, not touching the cylinder, but leaving about an inch or an inch and a half space between his hands and the projections. Soon the cylinder started to spin, and I was astounded as the thing picked up speed and was soon rotating at quite a merry rate. My Guide stopped it with a touch, and placed his hands in the opposite direction so that the fingers—instead of pointing away from his body as had been the case—now pointed toward his body. The cylinder started to spin but in the opposite direction! "You are blowing upon it!" I said. "Everyone says that!" said the Medical Lama Chinrobnobo, "but they are completely wrong."

The Great Medical Lama went to a recess in the far wall, and returned bearing a sheet of glass, it was quite a thick sheet, and he carried it carefully to my Guide the Lama Mingyar Dondup. My Guide stopped the cylinder from rotating and sat quiet while the Great Medical Lama Chinrobnobo placed the sheet of glass between my Guide and the paper cylinder. "Think about rotation," said the Medical Lama. My Guide apparently did so, for the cylinder started to rotate again. It was quite impossible for my Guide or for anyone else to have blown on the cylinder and made it rotate because of the glass. He stopped the cylinder again and then turned to me and said, "You try it, Lobsang!" He rose from his seat and I took his place.

I sat down and placed my hands just as had my Guide. The Medical Lama Chinrobnobo held the sheet of glass in front of me so that my breath would not influence the rotation of the cylinder. I sat there feeling like a fool. Apparently the cylinder thought I was one too, for nothing happened. "Think of making it rotate, Lobsang!" said my Guide. I did so, and immediately the thing started to go round. For a moment I felt like dropping everything and running—I thought the thing was bewitched, then reason (of a sort!) prevailed and I just sat still.

"That device, Lobsang," said my Guide, "runs by the force of the human aura. You think of rotating it and your aura puts a swirl on the thing which causes it to turn. You may be interested to know that a device such as this

162

has been experimented with in all the greater countries of the world. All the greatest scientists have tried to explain away the workings of this thing, but Western people, of course, cannot believe in etheric force and so they invent explanations which are even stranger than the actual force of the etheric!"

The Great Medical Lama said, "I am feeling quite hungry, Mingyar Dondup, I feel that it is time we repaired to our rooms for a rest and for sustenance. We must not tax the young man's abilities nor his endurance, for he will get enough of that in the future." We turned, and the lights were extinguished in that room, and we made our way up the stone corridor and into the main building of the Chakpori. Soon I was in a room with my Guide the Lama Mingyar Dondup. Soon—happy thought—I was consuming food and feeling the better for it. "Eat well, Lobsang," said my Guide, "for later in the day we shall see you again and discuss with you other matters."

For an hour or so I rested in my room, looking out of the window, because I had a weakness; I always liked to look from high places and watch the world moving beneath. I loved to watch the traders wending their slow way through the Western Gate, their every step indicating their delight at having reached the end of a long and arduous journey through the high mountain passes. Traders in the past had told me of the wonderful view there was from a certain spot on a high pass where, as one came from the Indian border, one could look down between a cleft in the mountains and gaze upon the Sacred City with its roof tops agleam with gold and, off by the side of the mountains, the white walls of "The Rice Heap," looking indeed like a heap of rice as it sprawled in bounteous profusion down the side of the mountainous slopes. I loved to watch the ferryman crossing the Happy River, and I hoped always for the sight of a puncture in his inflated hide boat, I longed to watch him gradually sink from sight until only his head protruded above the water. But I was

163

never that fortunate, the ferryman always reached the other side, took on his load, and returned again.

Soon, once more I was in that deep room with my Guide, the Lama Mingyar Dondup and the Great Medical Lama Chinrobnobo. "Lobsang!" said the great Medical Lama, "you must be sure that if you are going to examine a patient in order that you may assist him or her the clothes be entirely removed." "Honourable Medical Lama!" I said, in some confusion, "I can think of no reason why I should deprive a person of their clothing in this cold weather, for I can see their aura perfectly without there being any need whatsoever to remove a single garment, and oh! Respected Medical Lama! How could I possibly ask a woman to remove her clothing?" My eyes rolled upwards in horror at the mere thought. I must have presented quite a comical figure, for both my Guide and the Medical Lama burst out laughing. They sat down, and really enjoyed themselves with their laughter. I stood in front of them feeling remarkably foolish, but really, I was quite puzzled about these things. I could see an aura perfectly—with no trouble at all— and I saw no reason why I should depart from what was my normal practice.

"Lobsang!" said the Medical Lama, "you are a very gifted clairvoyant, but there are some things which you do not yet see. We have had a remarkable demonstration from you of your ability in seeing the human aura, but you would not have seen the liver complaint of the Indian Lama Marfata if he had not removed his clothing." I reflected upon this, and when I thought about it I had to admit that it was correct; I had looked at the Indian Lama while he had been robed, and while I had seen much about his character and basic traits, I still had not noticed the liver complaint. "You are perfectly correct, Honourable Medical Lama," I said, "but I should like some further training from you in this matter."

My Guide, the Lama Mingyar Dondup, looked at me and said, "When you look at a person's aura you want to see the person's aura, you are not concerned with the thoughts of the sheep whence came the wool which was made into a robe. Every aura is influenced by that which interferes with its direct rays. We have here a sheet of glass, and if I breathe upon that glass, it will effect what you see through the glass. Similarly, although this glass is transparent, it actually does alter the light or rather the colour of the light, which you would see when looking through it. In the same way, if you look through a piece of coloured glass all the vibrations which you receive from an object are altered in intensity by the action of the coloured glass. Thus it is that a person whose body has upon it clothing, or ornaments of any kind, has his aura modified according to the etheric content of the clothing or ornament." I thought about it, and I had to agree that there was quite a lot in what he said, he continued, "A further point is this, every organ of the body projects its own picture—its own state of health or sickness—onto the etheric, and the aura, when uncovered and free from the influence of clothes, magnifies and intensifies the impression which one receives. Thus it is quite definite that if you are going to help a person in health or in sickness, then you will have to examine him without his clothing." He smiled at me and said, "And if the weather be cold, why then, Lobsang, you will have to take him to a warmer place!"

"Honourable Lama," I said "some time ago you told me that you were working on a device which would enable one to cure illness through the aura." "That is perfectly correct, Lobsang," said my Guide, "illness is merely a dissonance in the body vibrations. An organ has its rate of molecular vibration disturbed and so it is considered to be a sick organ. If we could actually see how much the vibration of an organ departs from the normal, then, by restoring the rate of vibration to what it should be we have effected a cure. In the case of a mental affliction, the brain usually receives messages from the Overself which it cannot correctly interpret, and so the actions

165

resulting are those which depart from those which are accepted as normal actions for a human. Thus, if the human is not able to reason or act in a normal manner, he is said to have some mental ailment. By measuring the discrepancy—the under-stimulation—we can assist a person to recover normal balance. The vibrations may be lower than normal resulting in under-stimulation, or they may be higher than normal which would give an effect similar to that of a brain fever. Quite definitely illness can be cured by intervention through the aura."

The Great Medical Lama interrupted here, and said, "By the way, Respected Colleague, the Lama Marfata was discussing this matter with me, and he said that at certain places in India—at certain secluded lamaseries—they were experimenting with a very high voltage device known as a—" he hesitated and said, "it is a deGraaf generator." He was a bit uncertain about his terms, but he was making a truly manful effort to give us the exact information. "This generator apparently developed an extraordinarily high voltage at an extraordinarily low current; applied in a certain way to the body it caused the intensity of the aura to increase many many times so that even the non-clairvoyant could clearly observe it. I am told also that photographs have been taken of a human aura under these conditions." My Guide nodded solemnly, and said, "Yes, it is also possible to view the human aura by means of a special dye, a liquid which is sandwiched between two plates of glass. By arranging appropriate lighting and background, and viewing the nude human body through this screen many people can indeed see the aura."

I burst in and said, "But, Honourable Sirs! Why do people have to use all these tricks? I can see the aura—why cannot they?" My two mentors laughed again, this time they did not feel it necessary to explain the difference between training such as I had had and the training of the average man or woman in the street.

The Medical Lama said, "Now we probe in the dark,

166

we try to cure our patients by rule of thumb, by herbs and pills and potions. We are like blind men trying to find a pin dropped on the ground. I would like to see a small device so that any non-clairvoyant person could look through this device and see the human aura, see all the faults of the human aura, and, in seeing would be able to cure the discrepancy or the deficiency which truly was the cause of the illness."

For the rest of that week I was shown things by hypnotism and by telepathy, and my powers were increased and intensified, and we had talk after talk on the best ways to see the aura and to develop a machine which would also see the aura, and then, upon the last night of that week, I went to my little room in the Chakpori Lamasery and looked out of the window thinking that on the morrow I would return again to that bigger dormitory where I slept in company with so many others.

The lights in the Valley were atwinkle. The last dying rays peering over the rocky rim of our Valley glanced down, flicking the golden roofs as if with sparkling fingers, sending up showers of golden light, and in doing so breaking the light into iridescent colours which were of the spectrum of the gold itself. Blues and yellows and reds, and even some green struggled to attract the eye, growing dimmer and dimmer as the light faded. Soon the Valley itself was as encased in dark velvet, a dark blue-violet or purple velvet which could almost be felt. Through my open window I could smell the scent of the willows, and the scent of plants in the garden so far below me, a vagrant breeze wafted stronger scents to my nostrils, pollen, and budding flowers.

The last dying rays of the sun sank completely out of sight, no more did those probing fingers of light come over the edge of our rock-bound Valley, instead they shot off into the darkening sky, and reflected on low lying clouds showing red and blue. Gradually the night became darker as the sun sank further and further beyond our world. Soon there were bright specks of light in the dark purple sky, the light of Saturn, of Venus, of Mars. And then came the light of the Moon, hanging gibbous in the sky with all the pock marks showing plain and clear, and across the face of the Moon drifted a light fleecy cloud. It reminded me of a woman drawing a garment across herself after having been examined through her aura. I turned away, resolved in every fibre of my being that I would do all I could to increase the knowledge of the human aura, and to help those who went out into the great world and brought help and ease to suffering millions. I lay down upon the stone floor, and almost as soon as my head touched my folded robe I fell asleep and knew no more.

CHAPTER NINE

The silence was profound. The air of concentration intense. At long intervals there came an almost inaudible rustle which soon subsided again into death-like quiet. I looked about me, looking at the long lines of motionless robed figures sitting erect on the floor. These were intent men, men concentrating on the doings of the outside world. Some, indeed, were more concerned with the doings of the world *outside* this one! My eyes roamed about, dwelling first on one august figure, and then on another. Here was a great Abbot from a far-off district. There was a lama in poor and humble dress, a man come down from the mountains. Unthinkingly I moved one of the long, low tables so that I had more room. The silence was oppressive, a *living* silence, a silence that should not be, with so many men here.

Crash! The silence was rudely and loudly shattered. I jumped a foot off the ground, in a sitting position, and somehow spun round at the same time. Sprawled out at full length, still in a daze, was a Library messenger, with wooden-backed books still clattering around him. Coming in, heavily laden, he had not seen the table which I had moved. Being only eighteen inches from the ground it had effectively tripped him. Now it was on top of him.

Solicitous hands gently picked up the books and dusted them off. Books are revered in Tibet. Books contain knowledge and must never be abused or mishandled. Now the thought was for the books and not for the man. I picked up the table and moved it out of the way. Wonder of wonders, no one thought that I was in any way to blame! The messenger, rubbing his head, was trying to work out what happened. I had not been near; obviously

I could not have tripped him. Shaking his head in astonishment, he turned and went out. Soon calm was restored, and the lamas went back to their reading in the Library.

Having been damaged top and bottom (literally!) while working in the kitchens, I had been permanently banished therefrom. Now, for "menial" work I had to go to the great Library and dust the carvings on book covers and generally keep the place clean. Tibetan books are big and heavy. The wooden covers are intricately carved, giving the title and often a picture as well. It was heavy work, lifting the books from shelves, carrying them silently to my table, dusting them and then returning each book to its allotted place. The Librarian was very particular, carefully examining each book to see that it really was clean. There were wooden covers which housed magazines and papers from countries outside our boundaries. I liked particularly to look at these, although I could not read a single word. Many of these months-old foreign papers had pictures, and I would pore over them whenever possible. The more the Librarian tried to stop me, the more I delved into these forbidden books whenever his attention was taken from me.

Pictures of wheeled vehicles fascinated me. There were, of course, no wheeled vehicles in the whole of Tibet, and our Prophecies indicated most clearly that with the advent of wheels into Tibet there would be the "beginning of the end." Tibet would later be invaded by an evil force which was spreading across the world like a cancerous blight. We hoped that, in spite of the Prophecy, larger— more powerful nations — would not be interested in our little country which had no warlike intentions, no designs upon the living space of others.

I looked at pictures, and I was fascinated, on one magazine (of course I do not know what it was called). I saw some pictures—a whole series of them—which showed the magazine being printed. There were huge machines with great rollers and immense cog wheels. Men, in the pictures, were working like maniacs, and I thought

170

how different it was here in Tibet. Here one worked with the pride of craftsmanship, with the pride of doing a job well. No thought of commerce entered the mind of the craftsman of Tibet. I turned and looked at those pages again, and then I thought of how we were doing things.

Down in the Village of Shö books were being printed. Skilled monk-carvers were carving onto fine woods Tibetan characters, carving them with the slowness which ensured absolute accuracy, absolute fidelity to minute detail. After the carvers finished each board of print others would take that board and would polish it so that no flaw nor roughness remained on the wood, then the board would be taken away to be inspected by others for accuracy as to text, for no mistake was ever allowed to creep into a Tibetan book. Time did not matter, accuracy did.

With the boards all carved, all carefully polished and inspected for errors or flaws, it would pass to the monk-printers. They would lay the board face up on a bench, and then ink would be rolled onto the raised, carved words. Of course the words were all carved in reverse, so that when printed they would appear the right way round. With the board inked and carefully inspected once again to make sure that no portion was left uninked, a sheet of stiff paper akin to the papyrus of Egypt would be quickly spread across the type with its inked surface. A smooth rolling pressure would be applied to the back of the sheet of paper, and then it would be stripped off from the printing surface in one swift movement. Monk-inspectors would immediately take the page and examine it with minute care for any fault—any flaw—and if there was any flaw the paper would not be scrapped nor burned, but would be made up into bundles.

The printed word, in Tibet, is held as near-sacred, it is considered to be an insult to learning to destroy or mutilate paper which bears words of learning or religious words, thus in the course of time Tibet has accumulated bundle after bundle, bale after bale, of slightly imperfect sheets.

If the sheet of paper was considered satisfactorily printed, the printers were given the "go-ahead" and they went on producing various sheets each one of which was as carefully examined for flaws as was the first. I often used to watch these printers at work, and in the course of my studies I had to undertake their own work myself. I carved the printed words in reverse, I smoothed the carvings after, and under meticulous supervision I inked and later printed books.

Tibetan books are not bound as are Western books. A Tibetan book is a long affair, or perhaps it would be better to say it was a wide affair and very short, because a Tibetan line of print extends for several feet, but the page may be only a foot high. All the sheets containing the necessary pages would be carefully laid out and in the fulness of time—there was no hurry— they would dry. When they had been allowed time and time again for drying, the books would be assembled. First there would be a baseboard to which there were attached two tapes, then upon the baseboard would be assembled the pages of the book in their correct order, and when each book was thus assembled, upon the pile of printed pages would be placed another heavy board which formed the cover. This heavy board would bear intricate carvings, perhaps showing scenes from the book, and of course, giving the title. The two tapes from the bottom board would now be brought up and fastened across the top board, some considerable pressure would be exerted so that all the sheets were forced down into one compact mass. Particularly valuable books would then be carefully wrapped in silk and the wrappings would be sealed so that only those with adequate authority could open the wrapping and disturb the peace of that so carefully printed book!

It seemed to me that many of these Western pictures were of women in a remarkable state of undress; it occurred to me that these countries must be very hot countries, for how otherwise could women go about in such a scanty state? On some of the pictures people were lying down, obviously dead, while standing over them would be perhaps a villainous looking man with a piece of metal tubing in one hand from whence issued smoke. I never could understand the purpose of this, for—to judge from my own impressions—the people of the Western world made it their chief hobby to go round and kill each other, then big men with strange dresses on would come and put metal things on the hands, or wrists, of the person with the smoking tube.

The underclad ladies did not distress me at all, nor excite any particular interest in me, for Buddhists and Hindus, and, in fact, all the peoples of the East knew well that sex was necessary in human life. It was known that sexual experience was perhaps the highest form of ecstasy which the human could experience while still in the flesh. For that reason many of our religious paintings showed a man and a woman—usually referred to as God and Goddess— in the closet of close embraces. Because the facts of life, and of birth, were so well known there was no particular need to disguise what were facts, and so sometimes a detail was almost photograhpic. To us this was in no way pornographic, in no way indecent, but was merely the most convenient method of indicating that with the union of male and female certain specific sensations were generated, and it was explained that with the union of souls much greater pleasure could be experienced, but that, of course, would not be upon this world.

From talks with traders in the City of Lhasa, in the Village of Shö, and those who rested by the wayside at the Western Gate, I gathered the amazing information that in the Western world it was considered indecent to expose one's body to the gaze of another. I could not understand why this should be so, for the most elementary fact of life was that there had to be two sexes. I remembered a conversation with an old trader who frequented the route between Kalimpong in India and Lhasa.

Throughout some considerable time I had made it my business to meet him at the Western Gate, and to greet him at one more successful visit to our land. Often we would stand and chat for quite a while, I would give him news about Lhasa and he would give me news about the great world outside. Often, too, he would bring books and magazines for my Guide the Lama Mingyar Dondup, and I would then have the pleasant task of delivering them. This particular trader once said to me, "I have told you much about the people of the West, but I still do not understand them, one of their sayings in particular just does not make sense to me. It is this; Man is made in the image of God, they say, and yet they are afraid to show their body which they claim is made in the image of God. Does it mean, then, that they are ashamed of God's form?" He would look at me questioningly, and I of course was quite at a loss, I just could not answer his question. Man is made in the image of God. Therefore, if God is the ultimate in perfection—as should be the case—there should be no shame in exposing an image of God. We so-called heathens were not ashamed of our bodies, we knew that without sex there would be no continuation of the race. We knew that sex, on appropriate occasions, and in appropriate surroundings of course, increased the spirituality of a man and of a woman.

I was also astounded when I was told that some men and women who had been married, perhaps for years, had never seen the unclad body of the other. When I was told that they "made love" only with the blinds down and the light out I recall I thought my informant was taking me for a country bumpkin who really was too foolish to know what was going on in the world, and after one such session I decided that at the first opportunity I would ask my Guide, the Lama Mingyar Dondup, about sex in the Western world. I turned away from the Western Gate, and dashed across the road to the narrow, dangerous path which we boys of Chakpori used

174

in preference to the regular path. This path would have frightened a mountaineer; frequently it frightened us as well, but it was a point of honour not to use the other path unless we were in company with our seniors and, presumably, betters. The mode of progression upwards entailed climbing by hand up jagged "tooths" of rock, dangling precariously from certain exposed routes, and at all times doing those things which no presumably sane person would do if they were paid a fortune. Eventually I reached the top, and got into the Chakpori by a route which was also known to us and which would have given the Proctors fits if they too had known. So—at last I stood within the Inner Courtyard far more exhausted than if I had come up the orthodox path, but at least honour was satisfied. I had done the trip up somewhat faster than some of the boys did it down.

I shook the dust and small stones out of my robe, and emptied my bowl which had collected numerous small plants, and then feeling fairly presentable I wended my way inwards in search of my Guide, the Lama Mingyar Dondup. As I rounded a corner I saw him proceeding away from me and so I called, "Ow! Honourable Lama!" He stopped, and turned and walked towards me, an action which possibly no other man in Chakpori would have done, for he treated every man and boy as equal, as he used to say, it is not the outward form, it is not the body which one is at present wearing but what is inside—what is controlling the body—that counts. My Guide himself was a Great Incarnation who easily had been Recognised on his return to body. It was an always-remembered lesson for me that this great man was humble and always considered the feelings of those who were not merely "not so great", but some who were—to put it bluntly— downright low.

"Well now, Lobsang!" said my Guide, "I saw you coming up that forbidden path, and if I had been a Proctor you would have been smarting in quite a number of places now; you would have been glad to remain standing for

175

many hours." He laughed, and said, "However, I used to do substantially the same thing myself, and I still get what is possibly a forbidden thrill in seeing others do what I can no longer do. Well, what is the rush anyhow?" I looked up at him and said, "Honourable Lama, I have been hearing horrible things about the people of the Western world, and my mind is indeed in a constant turmoil, for I am unable to tell if I am being laughed at—if I am being made to look a worse fool than usual—or whether the marvels which have been described to me are indeed fact." "Come with me, Lobsang," said my Guide, "I am just going to my room, I was going to meditate, but let us discuss things instead. Meditation can wait." We turned and walked along side by side to the Lama Mingyar Dondup's room—the one which overlooked the Jewel Park. I entered the room in his footsteps, and instead of immediately sitting down, he rang for the attendant to bring us tea. Then, with me by his side, he moved across to the window and looked out across that lovely expanse of land. Land which was one of the most beautiful places perhaps in the whole world. Below us, slightly to our left, was the fertile, wooded garden known as the Norbu Linga or Jewel Park. The beautiful clear water sparkled among the trees, and the Inmost One's small Temple set upon an island was gleaming in the sunlight. Someone was crossing the rocky causeway—a path across the water made of flat stones with spaces between so that the water could flow free and the fish would have no bar. I looked carefully, and thought I could distinguish one of the high members of the Government. "Yes, Lobsang, he is going to see the Inmost One," said my Guide in answer to my unspoken thought. Together we watched for some time, for it was pleasant here looking out upon that park with, beyond it, The Happy River sparkling and dancing as if with the joy of a beautiful day. We could also see down by the Ferry, one of my favourite spots—it was a never ending source of pleasure and amaze-

176

ment to me to see the ferryman get on his inflated skin boat and paddle away merrily to the other side.

Below us, between us and the Norbu Linga, pilgrims were making their slow way along the Lingkor Road. They went along giving hardly a glance to our own Chakpori but keeping a constant lookout to see if possibly they could see anything of interest in the Jewel Park, for it must have been common knowledge to the ever-alert pilgrims that the Inmost One would be at the Norbu Linga. I could see too the Kashya Linga, a little park, well wooded, which was by the side of the Ferry Road. There was a small road leading from the Lingkor Road down to the Kyi Chu, and it was used mainly by travellers who wanted to use the Ferry. Some, however, used it to reach the Lamas' Garden which was on the other side of the Ferry Road.

The attendant brought in tea for us and pleasant food as well. My Guide, the Lama Mingyar Dondup, said, "Come, Lobsang, let us break our fast for men who are going to debate must not be empty inside unless their head also proves to be empty!" He sat down on one of the hard cushions which we of Tibet use instead of chairs, for we sit upon the floor crosslegged. So seated, he motioned for me to follow his example, which I did with alacrity because the sight of food was always one to make me hurry. We ate in comparative silence. In Tibet, particularly among monks, it was not considered seemly to speak or to make a noise while food was before us. Monks alone ate in silence, but if they were in a congregation of any great number a Reader would read aloud from the Sacred Books. This Reader would be in a high place where, in addition to seeing his book, he could look out across the gathering of monks, and see immediately those who were so engrossed with their food that they had no time for his words. When there was a congregation of monks eating, then Proctors also would be present to see that there was no talking except for the monk-Reader. But we were alone; we passed a few desultory remarks to each other, knowing that many of the old customs, such as remaining silent at meals, were good for discipline when one was in a throng, but were not necessary for just a pair such as we. So, in my conceit, I classed myself as an associate of one of the truly great men of my country. "Well Lobsang," said my Guide when we had finished our meal, "tell me what it is that bothers you so?"

"Honourable Lama!" I said in some excitement, "a trader passing through here, and with whom I was discussing matters of some moment at the Western Gate, gave me some remarkable information about the people of the West. He told me that they thought our religious paintings obscene. He told me some incredible things about their sex habits, and I am still not at all sure that he was not taking me for a fool." My Guide looked at me and thought for a moment or two, then he said, "To go into this matter, Lobsang, would take more than one session. We have to go to our Service and the time is near for that. Let us just discuss one aspect of this first, shall we?" I nodded, very eagerly, because I really was most puzzled about all this. My Guide then said, "All this springs from religion. The religion of the West is different from the religion of the East. We should look into this and see what bearing it has on the subject." He arranged his robes about him more comfortably, and rang for the attendant to clear the things from the table. When that had been done, he turned to me and started a discussion which I found to be of enthralling interest.

"Lobsang," he said, "we must draw a parallel between one of the religions of the West and our own Buddhist religion. You will realise from your lessons that the Teachings of our Lord Guatama have been altered somewhat in the course of time. Throughout the years and the centuries which have elapsed since the passing from this earth of The Guatama and His elevation to Buddhahood, the Teachings which He personally taught have changed. Some of us think they have changed for the worse. Others think that the Teachings have been brought into line with

178

modern thought." He looked at me to see if I was following him with sufficient attention, to see if I understood what he was talking about. I understood and I followed him perfectly. He nodded to me briefly and then continued.

"We had our Great Being whom we call Guatama, whom some call The Buddha. The Christians also had their Great Being. Their Great Being propounded certain Teachings. Legend and, in fact, actual records testify to the fact that their Great Being who, according to their own Scriptures, wandered abroad in the Wilderness, actually visited India and Tibet in search of information, in search of knowledge, about a religion which would be suitable for Western mentalities and spiritualities. This Great Being came to Lhasa and actually visited our Cathedral, The Jo Kang. The Great Being then returned to the West and formulated a religion which was in every way admirable and suitable for the Western people. With the Passing of that Great Being from this earth—as our own Guatama passed—certain dissensions arose in the Christian Church. Some sixty years after that Passing, a Convention, or Meeting, was held at a place called Constantinople. Certain changes were made in Christian dogma—certain changes were made in Christian belief. Probably some of the priests of the day felt that they had to put in a few torments in order to keep some of the more refractory of their congregation in good order." Again he looked at me to see if I was following him. Again I indicated that I was not merely following him, but that I was vastly interested.

"The men who attended that Convention at Constantinople in the year 60 were men who were not sympathetic toward women, just as some of our monks feel faint at at the mere thought of a woman. The majority of them regarded sex as something unclean, something which should only be resorted to in the case of absolute necessity in order to increase the race. These were men who had no great sexual urges themselves, no doubt they had

179

other urges, perhaps some of those urges were spiritual —I do not know—I only know that in the year 60 they decided that sex was unclean, sex was the work of the devil. They decided that children were brought into the world unclean and were not fit to go to a reward until in some way they had been cleansed first." He paused a moment and then smiled as he said, "I do not know what is supposed to happen to all the millions of babies born before this meeting at Constantinople!"

"You will understand, Lobsang, that I am giving you information about Christianity as I understand it. Possibly when you go to live among these people you will have some different impression or different information which may in some way modify my own opinions and teachings." As he finished his statement the conches sounded, and the temple trumpets blared. About us there was the ordered bustle of disciplined men getting ready for the Service. We too stood up and brushed off our robes before making our way down to the Temple for the Service. Before leaving me at the entrance, my Guide said, "Come to my room after, Lobsang, and we will continue our discussion." So I entered into the Temple and I took my place among my fellows, and I said my prayers and I thanked my own particular God that I was a Tibetan the same as my Guide, the Lama Mingyar Dondup. It was beautiful in the old Temple, the air of worship, the gently drifting clouds of incense which kept us in touch with people on other planes of existence. Incense is not just a pleasant smell, not something which "disinfects" a Temple—it is a living force, a force which is so arranged that by picking the particular type of incense we can actually control the rate of vibration. Tonight, in the Temple, the incense was floating and giving a mellow, old world atmosphere to the place. I looked out from my place among the boys of my group—looked out into the dim mists of the Temple building. There was the deep chanting of the old lamas accompanied by—at times—the silver bells. Tonight we had a Japanese monk with us. He had come all the way across our land after having stopped in India for some time. He was a great man in his own country, and he had brought with him his wooden drums, drums which play such a great part in the religion of the Japanese monks. I marvelled at the versatility of the Japanese monk, at the remarkable music he produced from his drums. It seemed truly amazing to me that hitting a sort of wooden box could sound so very musical; he had the wooden drum and he had sort of clappers, each with little bells attached, and also our own lamas accompanied him with silver bells, with the great temple conch booming out in appropriate time. It seemed to me that the whole Temple vibrated, the walls themselves seemed to dance and shimmer and the mists away in the distance of the far recesses seemed to form into faces, the faces of long-dead lamas. But for once all too soon, the Service had ended, and I hurried off as arranged to my Guide, the Lama Mingyar Dondup.

"You have not wasted much time, Lobsang!" said my Guide cheerfully. "I thought perhaps you would be stopping to have one of those innumerable snacks!" "No, Honourable Lama," I said, "I am anxious to get some enlightenment, for I confess the subject of sex in the Western world is one which has caused me a lot of astonishment after having heard so much about it from traders and others." He laughed at me and said, "Sex causes a lot of interest everywhere! It is sex, after all, which keeps people on this earth. We will discuss it as you require it so."

"Honourable Lama," I said, "you said previously that sex was the second greatest force in the world. What did you mean by that? If sex is so necessary in order to keep the world populated why is it not the most important force?" "The greatest force in the world, Lobsang," said my Guide, "is not sex, the greatest force of all is imagination, for without imagination there would be no sexual impulse. If a male had no imagination, then the male could not be interested in the female. Without imagination there would be no writers, no artists, there would be nothing whatever that was constructive or good!" "But, Honourable Lama," I said, "are you saying that imagination is necessary for sex? And if you are, how does imagination apply to animals?" "Imagination is possessed by animals, Lobsang, just as it is possessed by humans. Many people think that animals are mindless creatures, without any form of intelligence, without any form of reason, yet I, who have lived a surprisingly long number of years, tell you differently." My Guide looked at me, and then shaking a finger at me he said, "You profess to be fond of the Temple cats, are you going to tell me that they have no imagination? You always speak to the Temple cats, you stop to caress them. After you have been affectionate with them once they will wait for you a second time, and a third time, and so on. If this were mere insensitive reactions, if these were just brain patterns, then the cat would not wait for you on the second or third occasion, but would wait until the habit had been formed. No, Lobsang, any animal has imagination. An animal imagines the pleasures in being with its mate, and then the inevitable occurs!"

When I came to think about it, to dwell upon the subject, it was perfectly clear to me that my Guide was absolutely right. I had seen little birds—little hens—fluttering their wings in much the same way as young women flutter their eyelids! I had watched little birds and seen very real anxiety as they waited for their mates to return from the unceasing forage for food. I had seen the joy with which a loving little bird had greeted her mate upon his return. It was obvious to me, now that I thought about it, that animals really had imagination, and so I could see the sense of my Guide's remarks that imagination was the greatest force on earth.

"One of the traders told me that the more occult a person was the more he was opposed to sex, Honourable Lama," I said. "Is this true, or am I being teased? I have heard so many very strange things that I really do not know how I stand in the matter." The Lama Mingyar Dondup nodded sadly, as he replied, "It is perfectly true, Lobsang, that many people who are intensely interested in occult matters are intensely antipathetic to sex, and for a special reason; you have been told before that the greatest occultists are not normal, that is, they have something wrong with them physically. A person may have a grave disease, such as T.B., or cancer, or anything of that nature. A person may have some nerve complaint —whatever it is, it is an illness and that illness increases metaphysical perceptions." He frowned slightly as he continued, "Many people find that the sexual impulse is a great drive. Some people for one reason or another use methods of sublimating that sexual drive, and they may turn to things spiritual. Once a man or a woman has turned away from a thing they become a deadly enemy to that thing. There is no greater reformer—no greater campaigner—against the evils of drink than the reformed drunkard! In the same way, a man or a woman who has renounced sex (possibly because they could not satisfy nor be satisfied!) will turn to occult matters, and all the drive which formerly went (successfully or unsuccessfully) into sexual adventures is now devoted to occult adventures. But unfortunately these people so often tend to be unbalanced about it; they tend to bleat that only in renouncing sex is it possible to progress. Nothing could be more fantastic, nothing could be more distorted, some of the greatest people are able to enjoy a normal life and also to progress vastly in metaphysics."

Just at that moment the Great Medical Lama Chinrobnobo came in, we greeted him and he sat down with us. "I am just telling Lobsang some matters about sex and occultism," said my Guide. "Ah yes!" said the Lama Chinrobnobo, "it is time he was given some information on this; I have thought so for a long time." My Guide continued, "It is clear that those who use sex normally —as it is meant to be used—increase their own spiritual force. Sex is not a matter to be abused, but on the other

183

hand nor is it a matter to be repudiated. By bringing vibrations to a person that person can increase spiritually. I want to point out to you, however," he said looking sternly at me, "that the sexual act should only be indulged in by those who are in love, by those who are bound together by spiritual affinity. That which is illicit, unlawful, is mere prostitution of the body and can harm one as much as the other can help one. In the same way a man or a woman should have only one partner, eschewing all temptations which would lead one from the path of truth and righteousness."

The Lama Chinrobnobo said, "But there is another matter upon which you should dwell, Respected Colleague, and it is this, the matter referring to birth control. I will leave you to deal with it." He rose to his feet, bowed gravely to us and left the room.

My Guide waited for a moment, and then said, "Are you tired of this yet, Lobsang?" "No, Sir!" I replied, "I am anxious to learn all I can for all this is strange to me." "Then you should know that in the early days of life upon earth peoples were divided into families. Throughout areas of the world there were small families which, with the passage of time became big families. As seems to be inevitable among humans, quarrels and dissensions occurred. Family fought against family. The victors killed the men they had vanquished and took their women into their own family. Soon it became clear that the bigger the family, which was now referred to as a tribe, the more powerful and the more secure it was from the aggressive acts of others." He looked at me a bit ruefully, and then continued, "The tribes were increasing in size as the years and centuries went by. Some men set up as priests, but priests with a bit of political power, with an eye to the future! The priests decided that they had to have a sacred edict—what they could call a command from God—which would help the tribe as a whole. They taught that one had to be fruitful and multiply. In those days it was a very real necessity, because unless people

184

'multiplied' their tribe became weak and perhaps completely wiped out. So—the priests who commanded that the people be fruitful and multiply were even safeguarding the future of their own tribe. With the passage of centuries and centuries, however, it is quite clear that the population of the world is increasing at such a pace that the world is becoming over-populated, there are more people than food resources justify. Something will have to be done about it."

I could follow all this, it made sense to me, and I was glad to see that my friends of the Pargo Kaling—the traders who had travelled so far and for so long—had told me the truth.

My Guide continued, "Some religions even now think that it is wrong indeed to place any limitation upon the number of children who are born, but if one looks at world history one sees that most of the wars are caused by lack of living space on the part of the aggressor. A country has a rapidly expanding population, and it knows that if it goes on expanding at this rate there will not be enough food, not be enough opportunity, for those of its own peoples. Thus they make war, saying they have to have living space!" "Then, Honourable Lama," I said, "how would you deal with the problem?" "Lobsang!" he replied, "the matter is easy if men and women of goodwill get together to discuss the thing. The old forms of religions—the old religious teachings were in every way suitable when the world was young, when people were few, but now it is inevitable—and it will be in time!—that fresh approaches be made. You ask what I would do about it? Well, I would do this; I would make birth control legal. I would teach all peoples about birth control, how it could be accomplished, what it was, and all that could be discovered about it. I would see that those people who wanted children could have perhaps one or two, while those who did not want children had the knowledge whereby children would not be born. According to our religion, Lobsang, there would be no offence in doing this. I have studied the old books dating back long, long ages before life appeared on Western parts of this globe, for, as you know, life first appeared in China and in the areas around Tibet, and spread to India before going Westwards. However, we are not dealing with that."

I decided then and there that as soon as I could I would get my Guide to talk more about the origin of life upon this earth, but I recollected that now I was studying all I could on the matter of sex. My Guide was watching me, and as he saw that I was again paying attention he continued, "As I was saying, the majority of wars are caused by overpopulation. It is a fact that there will be wars—there will always be wars—so long as there are vast and increasing populations. And it is necessary that there should be for otherwise the world would be absolutely overrun with people in the same way that a dead rat is soon completely overrun by swarms of ants. When you move away from Tibet, where we have a very small population, and you go to some of the great cities of the world, you will be amazed and appalled at the vast numbers, at the vast throngs of people. You will see that my words are correct; wars are utterly necessary to keep down the population. People have to come to earth in order to learn things and unless there were wars and diseases, then there would be no way whatever of keeping the population in control and keeping them fed. They would be like a swarm of locusts eating everything in sight, contaminating everything, and in the end they would finish themselves up completely."

"Honourable Lama!" I said, "some of the traders who have talked about this birth control thing say that so many people think that it is evil. Now why should they think that?" My Guide thought for a moment, probably wondering how much he should tell me for I was as yet still young, and then he said, "Birth control to some appears to be murder of a person unborn, but in our Faith, Lobsang, the spirit has not entered the unborn baby. In our Faith no murder can possibly have occurred, and

186

anyhow it is, of course manifestly absurd to say that there is any murder in taking precautions to prevent conception. It is just as well to say that we murder a whole lot of plants if we prevent their seeds from germinating! Humans too often imagine that they are the most wonderful thing that ever happened in this great Universe. Actually, of course, humans are just one form of life, and not the highest form of life at that, however there is no time to go into such matters as that for the present."

I thought of another thing which I had heard, and it seemed to be such a shocking—such a terrible thing—that I could hardly bring myself to speak of it. However, I did! "Honourable Lama! I have heard that some animals, cows for instance, are made pregnant by unnatural means. Is that correct?" My Guide looked quite shocked for a moment, and then he said, "Yes, Lobsang, that is absolutely correct. There are certain peoples in the Western world who try to raise cattle by what they call artificial insemination, that is the cows are inseminated by a man with a great big syringe instead of having a bull do the necessary work. These people do not seem to realise that in making a baby, whether it be a baby human, a baby bear, or a baby cow, there is more than just a mechanical mating. If one is going to have good stock, then there must be love or a form of affection in the mating process. If humans were artificially inseminated, then it could be that—being born without love—they would be sub-humans! I repeat to you, Lobsang, that for the better type of human or beast it is necessary that the parents shall be fond of each other, that they shall both be raised in spiritual as well as physical vibration. Artificial insemination, carried out in cold, loveless conditions, results in very poor stock indeed. I believe that artificial insemination is one of the major crimes upon this earth."

I sat there, with the evening shadows stealing across the room, bathing the Lama Mingyar Dondup in the growing dusk, and as the dusk increased I saw his aura flaring with the great gold of spirituality. To me, clairvoyantly, the light was bright indeed and interpenetrated the dusk itself. My clairvoyant perceptions told me—as if I did not know before—that there I was in the presence of one of the greatest men of Tibet. I felt warm inside me, I felt my whole being throb with love for this, my Guide and tutor.

Beneath us the Temple conches blared again, but this time they were not calling us, but calling others. Together we walked to the window and looked out. My Guide put his hand on my shoulder as we looked out at the valley below us—the valley now partially enveloped in the purple darkness. "Let your conscience be your guide, Lobsang," said my Guide. "You will always know if a thing is right or if a thing is wrong. You are going far—farther than you can imagine—and you will have many temptations placed before you. Let your conscience be your guide. We in Tibet are a peaceful people, we are people of a small population, we are people who live in peace, who believe in holiness, who believe in the sanctity of the Spirit. Wherever you go, whatever you endure, let your conscience be your guide. We are trying to help you with your conscience. We are trying to give you extreme telepathic power and clairvoyance so that always in the future for so long as you live you can get in touch telepathically with great lamas here in the high Himalayas, great lamas who, later, will devote the whole of their time to waiting for your messages."

Waiting for my messages? I am afraid my jaw dropped with amazement; *my* messages? What was there so special about me? Why should great lamas be waiting for my messages all the time? My Guide laughed and slapped my shoulder. "The reason for your existence, Lobsang, is that you have a very, very special task to do. In spite of all the hardships, in spite of all the suffering, you will succeed in your task. But it is manifestly unfair that you should be left on your own in an alien world, a world that will mock you and call you a liar, fraud and fake. Never despair, never give up, for right will prevail. You—

Lobsang—will prevail!" The evening shadows turned into the darkness of night, below us the lights of the City were atwinkle. Above us a new moon was peeping down at us over the edge of the mountains. The planets, vast millions of them, twinkled in the purple heavens. I looked up, thought of all the forecasts about me—all the prophecies about me—and I thought also of the trust and the confidence shown by my friend, my Guide, the Lama Mingyar Dondup. And I was content.

CHAPTER TEN

The Teacher was in a bad mood; perhaps his tea had been too cold, perhaps his tsampa had not been roasted or mixed exactly to his liking. The Teacher was in a bad mood; we boys sat in the classroom just about shivering with fright. Already he had pounced unexpectedly upon boys to my right and boys to my left. My memory was good, I knew the Lessons perfectly—I could repeat chapter and verse from any part of the hundred and eight volumes of The Kangyur. *"Thwack! Thwack!!"* I jumped about a foot in the air with surprise, and about three boys to the left and three boys to the right also jumped a foot in the air with surprise. For a moment we hardly knew which of us was getting the hiding, then, as the Teacher laid it on a bit harder I knew that I was the unlucky one! He continued his beating, muttering all the time, "Lama's favourite! Pampered idiot!! I'll teach you to learn something." The dust rose from my robe in a choking cloud and started me sneezing. For some reason that enraged the Teacher even more, and he really worked up into knocking more dust out of me. Fortunately—unknown to him—I had anticipated his bad mood and had put on more clothes than usual, so—although he would not have been pleased to know it—his blows did not disturb me unduly. In any case I was hardened.

This Teacher was tyrannical. He was a perfectionist without being perfect himself. Not only did we have to be word-perfect in our Lesson Work, but if the pronunciation, the inflection, was not exactly to his desire he would take out his cane, whip round to the back, and then whip us on our backs. Now he was getting some exercise, and

190

I was nearly suffocating with the dust. Small boys in Tibet, like small boys everywhere, roll in the dust when they fight or when they play, and small boys completely cut off from all feminine influence do not always make sure that the dust is out of their clothing; mine was full of dust and this really was as good as a spring cleaning. The Teacher went on thwacking away, "I'll teach you to mispronounce a word! Showing disrespect to the Sacred Knowledge! Pampered idiot, always missing classes and then coming back and knowing more than the ones that I've taught—useless brat—I'll teach you, you'll learn from me one way or another!"

In Tibet we sit on the floor crosslegged, most times we sit on cushions which are about four inches thick, and in front of us we have tables which may be from twelve to eighteen inches from the ground, depending on the size of the student. This Teacher suddenly put his hand forcibly on the back of my head and pushed my head down onto my table where I had a slate and a few books. Having me in a suitable position, he took a deep breath and really got busy. I wriggled just from habit, not because I was being hurt, because in spite of his most earnest endeavours we boys were toughened, we were almost literally "tanned into leather," and things like this were just an everyday occurrence. Some boy made a soft chuckle six or seven boys away to the right, the Teacher dropped me as if I had suddenly glowed red hot and leapt like a tiger onto the other boy. I was careful to betray no indication of my own amusement when I saw a cloud of dust arising a few boys down the line! There were various exclamations of pain, fright, and horror from my right, because the Teacher was hitting out indiscriminately, not being at all sure which boy it was. At last, out of breath, and no doubt feeling a lot better, the Teacher stopped his exertions. "Ah!" he gasped, "that will teach you little horrors to pay attention to what I am saying. Now, Lobsang Rampa, start again and make sure that you get the pronunciation perfect." I commenced all over again, and when I thought about a thing I really could do it well enough. This time I thought—and then I thought again —so there were no more hard feelings from the Teacher and harder thwacks on me.

For the whole of that session, five hours in all, the Teacher paraded backwards and forwards keeping a very sharp eye indeed upon all of us, and no provocation at all was needed for him to lash out and catch some unlucky boy just when he thought he was unobserved. In Tibet we have our day starting at midnight, it starts then with a Service, and of course there are regular Services at regular intervals. Then we have to do menial work in order that we may be kept humble, in order that we shall not "look down" on the domestic staff. We also have a period of rest and after that we go to our classes. These classes last five hours non-stop, and during that whole time the teachers were indeed making us learn thoroughly. Our classes, of course, lasted more than five hours a day, but this particular session, the afternoon session, lasted five hours.

The hours dragged by, it seemed that we had been in that classroom for days. The shadows seemed scarcely to move and the sun overhead seemed as if rooted to one spot. We sighed in exasperation and with boredom, we felt that one of the Gods should come down and remove this particular Teacher from our midst, for he was the worst of them all, apparently forgetting that once, oh, so long ago! he too had been young. But at last, the conches sounded, and high above us on the roof a trumpet blared forth echoing across the Valley, sending an echo back from the Potala. With a sigh the Teacher said, "Well, I am afraid that I have to let you boys go now, but believe me when I see you again I shall make sure that you have learned something!" He gave a sign and motioned toward the door. The boys in the row nearest jumped to their feet and really bolted for it. I was just going as well but he called me back. "You, Tuesday Lobsang Rampa," he said, "you go away to your

Guide and you learn things, but don't come back here showing up the boys that I have taught, you are being taught by hypnotism and other methods, I am going to see if I cannot get you kicked out." He gave me a cuff to the side of the head, and continued, "Now get out of my sight, I hate the sight of you here, other people are complaining that you are learning more than the boys whom I teach." As soon as he let go of my collar I bolted too and did not even bother to shut the door behind me. He bawled out something but I was travelling too fast to go back.

Outside some of the other boys were waiting, well out of earshot of the Teacher of course. "We ought to do something about that one," said one boy. "Yes!" said another, "somebody is going to get really hurt if he goes on unchecked like that." "You, Lobsang," said a third boy, "you are always boasting about your Teacher and Guide, why don't you say something about the way we are ill-treated?" I thought about it, and it seemed to me to be a good idea, for we had to learn but there was no reason why we should be taught with such brutality. The more I thought about it the more pleasant it seemed; I would go to my Guide and tell him how we were treated, and he would go down and put a spell on this Teacher and turn him into a toad or something like that. "Yes!" I exclaimed, "I will go now." With that I turned and ran off.

I hastened along the familiar corridors, ascending up and up so that I got nearer the roof. At last I turned into the Lamas' Corridor and found that my Guide was already in his room with the door open. He bade me enter and said, "Why, Lobsang! You are in a state of excitement. Have you been made an abbot or something?" I looked at him rather ruefully, and said, "Honourable Lama, why are we boys so ill-treated in class?" My Guide looked at me quite seriously and said, "But how have you been treated badly, Lobsang? Sit down and tell me what it is that is worrying you so much."

I sat down, and commenced my sad recital. During the time I was speaking, my Guide made no comment, made no interruption whatever. He allowed me my say, and at last I reached the end of my tale of woe and almost the end of my breath. "Lobsang," said my Guide, "does it occur to you that life itself is just a school?" "A school?" I looked at him as if he had suddenly taken leave of his senses. I could not have been more surprised if he had told me that the sun had retired and the moon had taken over! "Honourable Lama," I said in astonishment, "did you say that life was a school?" "Most certainly I did, Lobsang, rest awhile, let us have tea, and then we will talk."

The attendant who was summoned soon brought us tea and enjoyable things to eat. My Guide partook of food very sparingly indeed. As he once said, I ate enough to keep about four of him! But he said it with such a twinkling smile that there was no offence implied or taken. He often teased me and I knew that he would never under any consideration say anything that would hurt another person. I really did not mind in the least what he said to me, knowing how well he meant it. We sat and had our tea, and then my Guide wrote a little note and gave it to the attendant to deliver to another Lama. "Lobsang, I have said that you and I will not be at Temple Service this evening, for we have much to discuss, and although Temple Services are very essential things, so—in view of your special circumstances—is it necessary to give you more tuition than average."

He rose to his feet and walked across to the window. I scrambled to my feet too and went across to join him, for it was one of my pleasures to look and see all that was happening, for my Guide had one of the higher rooms at the Chakpori, a room from which one could look out over wide spaces and see for long distances. Besides, he had that most enjoyable of all things, a telescope. The hours I spent with that instrument! The hours I spent looking away across the Plain of Lhasa, looking at the traders in the City itself, and watching the ladies of Lhasa going about their business, shopping, visiting, and just (as I put it) plain wasting time. For ten or fifteen minutes we stood there looking out, then my Guide said, "Let us sit down again, Lobsang, and discuss this matter about a school, shall we?

"I want you to listen to me, Lobsang, for this is a matter which you should have clear from the start. If you do not fully understand what I say then stop me immediately, for it is essential that you understand all this, you hear?" I nodded to him, and then as a matter of politeness said, "Yes, Honourable Lama, I hear you and I understand. If I do not understand I will tell you." He nodded and said, "Life is like a school. When we are beyond this life in the astral world, before we come down into a woman's body, we discuss with others what we are going to learn. Sometime ago I told you a story about Old Seng, the Chinaman. I told you that we would use a Chinese name because you, being you! would try to associate any Tibetan name with a Tibetan of your acquaintance. Let us say that Old Seng who died and saw all his past decided that he had certain lessons to learn. Then, the people who were helping him would look about to find parents, or, rather, prospective parents, who were living in the circumstances and in the conditions which would enable the soul which had been Old Seng to learn the desired lessons." My Guide looked at me and said, "It is much the same as a boy who is going to become a monk, if he wants to become a medical monk he comes to the Chakpori. If he wants to do perhaps domestic work, then no doubt he can get into the Potala for they always seem to have a shortage of domestic monks there! We choose our school according to what we want to learn." I nodded, because that was quite clear to me. My own parents had made arrangements for me to get into the Chakpori provided I had the necessary staying power to pass the initial test of endurance.

My Guide, the Lama Mingyar Dondup continued, "A

195

person who is going to be born already has everything arranged; the person is going to come down and be born of a certain woman who lives in a certain district and who is married to a certain class of man. It is thought that that will give the baby to be born the opportunities for gaining the experience and knowledge previously planned. Eventually, in the fulness of time, the baby is born. First the baby has to learn to feed, it has to learn how to control certain parts of its physical body—it has to learn how to speak and how to listen. At first, you know, a baby cannot focus its eyes, it has to learn how to see. It is at school." He looked at me and there was a smile on his face as he said, "None of us like school, some of us have to come, but others of us do not have to come. We plan to come—not for karma—but to learn other things. The baby grows up and becomes a boy and then goes to a classroom where often he gets treated rather roughly by his teacher, but there is nothing wrong in that, Lobsang. No one has ever been harmed by discipline. Discipline is the difference between an army and a rabble. You cannot have a cultured man unless that man has been disciplined. Many times now you will think that you are ill-treated, that the teacher is harsh and cruel, but—whatever you think now—you particularly arranged to come to this earth in these conditions." "Well, Honourable Lama," I explained excitedly, "if I arranged to come down here, then I think that I should have my brains examined. And if I arranged to come down here, why do I know nothing at all about it?"

My Guide looked at me and laughed—laughed outright. "I know just how you feel, Lobsang, today," he replied, "but really there is nothing that you should worry about. You came to this earth first to learn certain things. Then, having learned those certain things, you are going out into the greater world beyond our borders to learn other things. The Way will not be easy; but you will succeed in the end, and I do not want you to be despondent. Every person, no matter his station in life, has come down to earth from the astral planes in order that he may learn and, in learning, progress. You will agree with me, Lobsang, that if you want to progress in the Lamasery you study and pass examinations. You would not think much of a boy who was suddenly placed over you and by favouritism alone became a lama or an abbot. So long as there are proper examinations then you know that you are not being passed over at some superior person's whim or fancies or favouritisms." I could see that too, yes, when it was explained, it was quite a simple matter.

"We come to earth to learn things, and no matter how hard or how bitter the lessons which we learn on this earth, they are lessons for which we have enrolled before we came here. When we leave this earth we have our vacation for a time in the Other World, and then if we want to make progress we move on. We may return to this earth under different conditions, or we may move on to a completely different stage of existence. Often when we are in school we think that there is going to be no end to the day, we think that there is going to be no end to the harshness of the teacher. Life on earth is like that, if everything went smoothly for us, if we had everything that we wanted we should not be learning a lesson, we should just be drifting along on the stream of life. It is a sad fact that we only learn with pain and suffering." "Well then, Honourable Lama," I said, "why is it that some boys, and some lamas too, have such an easy time? It always appears to me that I get hardships, bad prophecies, and beatings-up by an irritable teacher when I really have done my best." "But, Lobsang, some of these people who apparently are very self-satisfied—are you sure that they are so self-satisfied? Are you sure that conditions are so easy for them, after all? Until you know what they planned to do before they came to the earth you are not in a position to judge. Every person coming to this earth comes with a prepared plan, a plan of what they want to learn, what they propose to do, and what they aspire to be when they leave this earth after sojourning in its school. And you say that you tried really hard at class today. Are you *sure*? Were you not rather complacent, thinking that you knew all there was to know about the lesson? Did you not, by your rather superior attitude, make the Teacher feel rather bad?" He looked at me somewhat accusingly, and I felt my cheeks grow somewhat red. Yes, he really knew something! My Guide had the most unhappy knack of putting his hand on a spot which was tender. Yes, I had been complacent, I had thought that this time the Teacher would not be able to find the slightest fault with me. My own superior attitude had, of course, in no small measure contributed toward the exasperation of that Teacher. I nodded in agreement, "Yes, Honourable Lama, I am as much to blame as anyone." My Guide looked at me, smiled, and nodded in approval.

"Later, Lobsang, you will be going to Chungking in China, as you know," said the Lama Mingyar Dondup. I nodded, dumbly, not liking even to think of the time when I should have to leave. He continued, "Before you leave Tibet we shall send to various colleges and universities for details about their instruction. We shall receive all particulars and we shall then decide which college or university will offer you exactly the type of training which you will need in this life. In a similar manner, before a person in the astral world even thinks of coming down to earth he weighs up what he proposes to do, what he wants to learn, and what he finally wants to achieve. Then, as I have already told you, suitable parents are discovered. That is the same as looking for a suitable school."

The more I thought about this school idea the more I disliked it. "Honourable Lama!" I said, "why do some people have so much illness, so much misfortune, what does that teach them?" My Guide said, "But you must remember that a person who comes down to this world has much to learn, it is not just a matter of learning to carve, not just a matter of learning a language or reciting from Sacred Books. The person has to learn things which are going to be of use in the astral world after leaving the earth. As I have told you, this is The World of Illusion, and it is extremely well suited to teach us hardship, and in suffering hardship, we should learn to understand the difficulties and the problems of others." I thought about all this, and it seemed that we had got onto a very big subject. My Guide obviously got my thoughts, for he said, "Yes, the night is coming upon us, it is time to end our discussion for this night for we have much to do yet. I have to go across to The Peak (as we called the Potala) and I want to take you with me. You will be there all night and all tomorrow. Tomorow we can discuss this matter again, but go now and put on a clean robe and bring a spare with you." He rose to his feet and left the room. I hesitated but for a moment—and that because I was in a daze!—and then I hurried off to array myself in my best, and to get my second best as my spare.

Together we jogged down the mountain road and into the Mani Lhakhang, just as we passed the Pargo Kaling, or Western Gate, there was a sudden loud squall behind me that almost lifted me from my saddle. "Ow! Holy Medical Lama!" yelled a feminine voice just to the side of the road. My Guide looked about him, and dismounted. Knowing my own uncertainties on a pony he motioned for me to remain seated, a concession which filled me with gratitude. "Yes, madam, what is it?" asked my Guide in kind tones. There was a sudden blur of movement, and a woman flung herself to the ground at his feet. "Oh! Holy Medical Lama!" she said breathlessly, "my husband could not beget a normal son, the misbegotten son of a she-goat!" Dumbly —stunned at her own audacity—she held out a small bundle. My Guide stooped down from his great height and looked. "But, madam!" he remarked, "why do you blame your husband for your ailing child?" "Because that ill-favoured man was always running around with loose women, all he thinks about is the opposite sex, and then when we get married he cannot even father a normal child." To my dismay she started weeping and her tears ran down to hit the ground with little plops, just like hailstones, I thought, coming down from the mountains.

My Guide looked about him, peering somewhat in the

increasing darkness. A figure by the side of the Pargo Kaling detached himself from the darker shadows and moved forward, a man in a ragged dress and wearing a definitely hang-dog expression. My Guide beckoned to him and he came forward, and knelt on the ground at the feet of the Lama Mingyar Dondup. My Guide looked at both of them and said, "You do not do right to blame each other for a mishap of birth, for this is not a matter which occurred between you, but is a matter to do with karma." He looked at the child again, pulling aside the wrappings in which the baby was swaddled. He looked hard, and I knew that he was looking at the infant's aura. Then he stood up saying, "Madam! Your child can be cured, his cure is well within our abilities. Why did you not bring him to us earlier?" The poor woman dropped to her knees again, and hastily passed the child to her husband, who took it as if it might explode at any moment. The woman clasped her hands, and looking at my Guide said, "Holy Medical Lama, who would pay attention to us, for we come from the Ragyab and we are not in favour with some of the other lamas. We could not come, Holy Lama, no matter how urgent our need."

I thought all this was ridiculous, the Ragyab or Disposers of the Dead, who lived in the South-East corner of Lhasa were as essential as any in our community. I knew that because my Guide was always stressing that no matter what a person did that person was still a useful member of the community. I remembered once laughing heartily when he said, "Even burglars, Lobsang, are useful people, for without burglars there would be no need of policeman, hence burglars provide policemen with employment!" But these Ragyab; many people looked down upon them thinking they were unclean because they dealt with the dead, cutting up dead bodies so that the vultures would eat the scattered pieces. I knew—and felt as my Guide—that they did good work, for much of Lhasa was so rocky, so stony, that graves could not be dug, and even if they could, normally Tibet was so cold that the bodies would just freeze and would not decay and be absorbed into the ground.

"Madam!" commanded my Guide, "you shall bring this child to me in person three days from now, and we shall do our utmost to see that he is cured, for from this brief examination it appears that he can be cured." He fumbled in his saddlebag and produced a piece of parchment. Quickly he wrote a message upon it, and handed it to the woman. "Bring that to me at the Chakpori and the attendant will see that you are admitted. I shall inform the gatekeeper that you are coming and you will have no difficulty whatever. Rest assured, we are all humans in the sight of our Gods, you have nothing to fear with us." He turned and looked at the husband; "You should remain loyal to your wife." He looked at the wife and added, "You should not abuse your husband so much, perhaps if you were kinder to him he would not go elsewhere for solace! Now, go to your home and in three days from now return here to the Chakpori and I will see you and assist you. That is my promise." He mounted his pony again and we rode off. Diminishing in the distance were the sounds of praises and thanks from the man of the Ragyab and his wife. "I suppose for tonight at least, Lobsang, they will be in accord, they will be feeling kindly disposed to each other!" He gave a short laugh and led the way up to the road to the left just before we reached the Village of Shö.

I really was amazed at this which was one of my first sights of husband and wife. "Holy Lama," I exclaimed, "I do not understand why these people came together if they do not like each other, why should that be?" My Guide smiled at me as he replied, "You are now calling me 'Holy Lama'! Do you think you are a peasant? As for your question, well we are going to discuss all that on the morrow. Tonight we are too busy. Tomorrow we will discuss these things and I will try to set your mind at rest, for it is sorely confused!" Together we rode up the hill. I always liked to look back down on the Village of Shö, and I wondered what would happen if I tossed a good sized pebble onto a roof or two; would it go through? Or would the clatter bring someone out thinking that the Devils were dropping something on them? I had never actually dared drop a stone down because I did not want it to go through the roof and through someone inside. However, I was always sorely tempted.

In the Potala we mounted the endless ladders—not stairways—ladders which were well-worn and steep, and at last we reached our apartments high up above the ordinary monk, above the storehouses. The Lama Mingyar Dondup went to his own room and I went to mine which was adjoining, by virtue of my Guide's position and by being his chela I had been allowed this room. Now I went to the window and as was my wont I looked out. Below us there was some night bird calling to its mate in the Willow Grove. The moon was bright now, and I could see this bird—see the ripples of water as its long legs stirred up water and mud. From somewhere in the quite near distance there came the answering call of a bird. "At least that husband and wife seem to be in harmony!" I thought to myself. Soon it was time to go to sleep for I had to attend the midnight Service, and already I was so tired that I thought that possibly in the morning I could oversleep.

In the afternoon of the next day the Lama Mingyar Dondup came into my room where I was studying an old book. "Come in with me, Lobsang," he said. "I have just returned from a talk with the Inmost One and now we have to discuss problems which are puzzling you." He turned and led the way into his own room. Sitting in front of him I thought of all the things which were on my mind. "Sir!" I said, "why are people who marry so unfriendly to each other? I looked at the aura of those two Ragyab last night, and it seemed to me that they really hated each other; if they hated each other why did they marry?" The Lama looked really sad for a few moments, and then he said, "People forget, Lobsang, that they come down to this earth in order to learn lessons. Before a person is born, while a person is still on the other side of life, arrangements are going ahead deciding what sort, what type, of marriage partner will be chosen. You should understand that a lot of people get married in what one might term the heat of passion. When passion spends itself, then the newness, the strangeness, wears off and familiarity breeds contempt!"

"Familiarity breeds contempt." I thought about it and thought about it. Why, then, did people get married? Obviously people got married in order that the race might continue. But why could not people get together the same as animals did? I raised my head and asked that question of my Guide. He looked at me and said, "Why, Lobsang! You surprise me, you should know as well as anyone that the so-called animals often mate for life. Many animals mate for life, many birds mate for life, certainly the more evolved ones do. If people got together, as you say, just for the purpose of increasing the race, then the resulting children would be almost soulless people, the same in fact as those creatures who are born by what is known as artificial insemination. There must be love in intercourse, there must be love between the parents if the best type of child is to be born, otherwise it is much the same as just a factory-made article!"

This business of husband and wife really puzzled me. I thought of my own parents, my Mother had been a domineering woman, and my Father had been really harsh to us, his children. I could not summon up much filial affection when I thought of either my Mother or my Father. I said to my Guide, "But why do people get married in the heat of passion? Why do they not get married as a business proposition?" "Lobsang!" said my Guide, "that is often the way of the Chinese and of the Japanese too. Their marriages are often arranged, and I must admit that Chinese and Japanese marriages are far far more successful than marriages in the Western world. The Chinese themselves liken it to a kettle. They do not marry in passion because they say it is like a kettle boiling and cooling off. They marry coolly and allow the mythical kettle to

203

come up to the boil, and in that way it stays hot longer!" He looked at me to see if I was following—to see if the matter was clear to me. "But I cannot see, Sir, why people are so unhappy together." "Lobsang, people come to earth as to a classroom, they come to learn things, and if the average husband and wife were ideally happy together then they would not learn, for there would be nothing to learn. They come to this earth to be together and to get on together—that is part of the lesson—they have to learn to give and to take. People have rough edges, edges or idiosyncrasies which jar and grate on the other partner. The grating partner must learn to subdue and perhaps end the annoying trait, while the partner who is annoyed must learn tolerance and forbearance. Almost any couple could live together successfully provided they learned this matter of give and take."

"Sir!" I said, "how would husband and wife be advised to live together?" "Husband and wife, Lobsang, should wait for a favourable moment, and should then kindly, courteously, and calmly say what is causing them distress. If a husband and a wife would discuss things together, then they would be more happy in their marriage." I thought about this, and I wondered how my Father and my Mother would get on if they tried to discuss anything together! To me they seemed to be fire and water, with each one being as antipathetic to the other. My Guide obviously knew what I was thinking for he continued, "There must be some give and take, because if these people are going to learn anything at all, then they should be sufficiently aware to know that there is something wrong with them." "But how is it," I asked, "that one person falls in love with another, or feels attracted to another? If they are attracted to each other at one stage why do they so soon cool off?" "Lobsang, you will well know that if one sees the aura one can tell about another person. The average person does not see the aura, but instead many people have a feeling, they can say that they like this person, or that they dislike that person. Most times they cannot say why they like or dislike, but they will agree that one person pleases them and another person displeases them." "Well, Sir," I exclaimed, "how can they suddenly like a person and then suddenly dislike a person?" "When people are at a certain stage, when they feel that they are in love, their vibrations are increased, and it may well be that when these two people, some man and some woman, have heightened vibrations they would be compatible. Unfortunately they do not always let them remain heightened. The wife will become dowdy, perhaps she will refuse the husband what is undeniably his right. The husband will then go out after some other woman, and gradually they will drift apart. Gradually their etheric vibrations will alter so that they are no longer compatible, so that they are completely antipathetic." Yes I could see that, and it really did explain much, but now I returned to the attack!

"Sir! I am most puzzled to know why a baby should live for perhaps a month and then die, what chance does that baby have of learning or paying back karma? It seems just a waste to everyone so far as I can see!" The Lama Mingyar Dondup smiled slightly at my vehemence. "No, Lobsang, nothing is wasted! You are being confused in your mind. You are assuming that a person lives for one life only. Let us take an example." He looked at me and then looked out of the window for a moment, I could see that he was thinking of those people of the Ragyab— thinking perhaps of their baby.

"I want you to imagine that you are accompanying a person who is getting through a series of lives," said my Guide. "The person has done rather badly in one life, and in later years that person decides that he cannot go on any longer, he decides that conditions are just too bad for him, so he puts an end to his life; he commits suicide. The person therefore died before he should have died. Every person is destined to live for a certain number of years, days and hours. It is all arranged before they come down to this earth. If a person terminates his own life perhaps twelve months before he would normally have died, then he has to come back and serve the additional twelve months." I looked at him and visualised some of the remarkable possibilities which could come from that. My Guide continued, "A person ends his life. He remains in the astral world until an opportunity occurs whereby he can come down to earth again under appropriate conditions and live out the time he has to serve on earth. This man with twelve months, well, he may come down and be a sickly baby, and he will die while he is still a baby. In losing that baby the parents also will have gained something; they will have lost a baby but they will have gained experience, they will have paid back a little of what they had to pay back. We will agree that while people are on earth their outlook, their perceptions, their values—everything—are distorted. This, I repeat, is the World of Illusion, the world of false values, and when people return to the Greater World of the Overself then they can see that the hard, senseless lessons and experiences undergone during this sojourn on earth were not so senseless after all."

I looked about me and thought of all the prophecies about me; prophecies of hardship, prophecies of torture, prophecies of sojourns in far and strange lands. I remarked, "Then a person who makes a prophecy is merely getting in touch with the source of information; if everything is arranged before one comes down to earth, then it is possible under certain conditions to tap that knowledge?" "Yes, that is perfectly correct," said my Guide, "but do not think that everything is laid out as inevitable. The basic lines are there. We are given certain problems, certain lines to follow, and then we are left to do the best we can. One person can make good and another person can fail. Look at it in this way; supposing two men are told that they have to go from here to Kalimpong in India. They do not have to follow the same path, but they have to arrive at the same destination if they can. One man will take one route and another man will take another route, depending upon the route which they take so will their experiences and adventures be affected. That is like life, our destination is known but how we get to that destination remains within our own hands."

As we were talking a messenger appeared, and my Guide, with a short word of explanation to me, followed the messenger down the corridor. I wandered again to the window, and rested my elbows on the ledge, supporting my face in my hands. I thought of all that I had been told, thought of all the experiences that I had had, and my whole being welled with love for that great man, the Lama Mingyar Dondup, my Guide, who had shown me more love than my parents had ever shown me. I decided that no matter what the future would bring, I would always act and behave as if my Guide were by my side supervising my actions. Down in the fields below monk musicians were practising their music; there were various "brumps-brumps-brumps" and squeaks and groans from their instruments. Idly I looked at them, music meant nothing to me for I was tone deaf, but I saw that they were very earnest men trying hard indeed to produce good music. I turned away thinking that I would occupy myself once again with a book.

Soon I tired of reading; I was unsettled. Experiences were tumbling upon me faster and faster. More and more idly I turned the pages, then, with sudden resolution I put all those printed sheets back between the carved wooden covers and tied the tapes. This was a book which had to be wrapped in silk. With inborn care I completed my task and set aside the book.

Rising to my feet I went to the window and looked out. The night was somewhat stuffy, still, with not a breath of wind. I turned, and left the room. All was still, still with the quietness of a great building which was almost alive. Here in the Potala men had worked at sacred tasks for some centuries and the building itself had developed life of its own. I hurried along to the end of the corridor and scaled a ladder there. Soon I emerged on to the high roof, by the side of the Sacred Tombs.

Silently I padded across to my accustomed spot, a spot which was well sheltered from the winds which normally raced down from the mountains. Lying back against a Sacred Image, with my hands clasped at the back of my head, I stared out across the Valley. Tiring of that after a time, I lay back and looked up at the stars. As I watched I had the strangest impression that all those worlds above were wheeling around the Potala. For a time it made me feel quite dizzy, as if I were falling. As I watched there was a thin tracery of light. Becoming brighter, it exploded into a sudden burst of brilliant light. "Another comet finished!" I thought, as it burned itself out and expired into a shower of dull red sparks.

I became aware of an almost inaudible "shush-shush" somewhere close by. Cautiously I raised my head, wondering what it could be. By the faint starlight I saw a hooded figure pacing backwards and forwards at the opposite side of the Sacred Tombs. I watched. The figure moved across to the wall facing the City of Lhasa. I saw the profile as he looked into the distance. The loneliest Man in Tibet I thought. The Man with more cares and responsibilities than anyone else in the country. I heard a deep sigh and wondered if He too had had hard prophecies such as I. Carefully I rolled over and crawled silently away; I had no desire to intrude—even innocently—upon the private thoughts of another. Soon I regained the entrance, and made my quiet way down to the sanctuary of my own room.

Some three days later I was present as my Guide, the Lama Mingyar Dondup examined the child of the Ragyab couple. He undressed it and carefully viewed the aura. For some time he pondered upon the base of the brain. This baby did not cry or whimper, no matter what my Guide did. As I knew, small as it was, it understood that the Lama Mingyar Dondup was trying to get it well. My Guide at last stood up, and said. "Well, Lobsang! we are going to get him cured. It is clear that he has an affliction caused by birth difficulties."

The parents were waiting in a room near the entrance. I, as close to my Guide as his shadow, went with him to see those people. As we entered they prostrated themselves at the Lama's feet. Gently he spoke to them; "Your son can and will be cured. From our examination it is clear that at the time of birth he was dropped or knocked. That can be remedied; you need have no fear." The mother trembled as she replied, "Holy Medical Lama, it is as you say. He came unexpectedly, suddenly, and was tumbled upon the floor. I was alone at the time." My Guide nodded in sympathy and understanding; "Return at this hour tomorrow and I am sure you will be able to take your child with you—cured." They were still bowing and prostrating themselves as we left the room.

My Guide made me examine the baby carefully. "Look, Lobsang, there is pressure here," he instructed. "This bone is pressing upon the cord—you observe how the auric light becomes fan shaped instead of round." He took my hands in his and made me feel round the affected area. "I am going to reduce, to *press out*, the obstructing bone. Watch!" Faster than I could see, he pressed his thumbs in—out. The baby made no outcry; it had been too fast for him to have felt pain. Now, though, the head was not lolling sideways as before, but was upright as a head should be. For some time my Guide massaged the child's neck, carefully from the head down towards the heart, and *never* in the opposite direction.

On the following day, at the appointed hour, the parents returned and were almost delirious with joy at seeing the seeming-miracle. "You have to pay for this," smiled the Lama Mingyar Dondup; "you have received good. Therefore you must *pay* good to each other. Do not quarrel nor be at variance with each other, for a child absorbs the attitudes of the parents. The child of unkind parents becomes unkind. The child of unhappy, loveless parents is unhappy and loveless in its turn. Pay—by kindness and love to each other. We will call upon you to see the child

209

in a week's time." He smiled, and patted the baby's cheek and then turned and went out, with me by his side.

"Some of the very poor people are proud, Lobsang, they are upset if they have not money with which to pay. Always make it possible for them to *think* they are paying." My Guide smiled as he remarked, "I told them they must pay. That pleased them, for they thought that, in their best dress, they had so impressed me that I thought they were people with money. The only way they can pay is as I said, by kindness to each other. Let a man and woman keep their pride, their self-respect, Lobsang, and they will do anything you ask!"

Back in my own room I picked up the telescope with which I had been playing. Extending the shining brass tubes I peered in the direction of Lhasa. Two figures came quickly into focus, one carrying a baby. As I watched, the man put an arm around his wife's shoulder and kissed her. Silently I put away the telescope and got on with my studies.

CHAPTER ELEVEN

We were having fun, several of us were out in the court-yard strutting around on our stilts, attempting to topple each other over. The one who could remain on the stilts impervious to the assaults of the others was the winner. Three of us subsided in a laughing heap, someone had put his stilts in a hole in the ground and bumped into us, tripping us. "Old Teacher Raks was in a blue mood today all right!" said one of my companions, happily. "Yes!" cried another of the heap, "it should make one of the others go green with envy that he could get in such a mood and take it out on us without getting out of breath." We all looked at each other and started to laugh; a blue mood? Green with envy? We called the others to come off their stilts and sit on the ground with us, and then we started a new game. How many colours could we use in describing things? "Blue in the face!" exclaimed one. "No," I answered, "we have already had blue, we have already had a blue mood." So we went on, working up from a blue mood to an abbot who was in a brown study, and a teacher who was green with envy. Another referred to a scarlet woman he had seen in the market place in Lhasa! For the moment we did not know if that would apply be-cause none of us were sure of what a scarlet woman was meant to be. "I know!" retorted the boy to my right, "we can have a man who is yellow, he is yellow with coward-ice. After all, yellow is often used to indicate cowardice." I thought about all this, and it seemed to me that if such sayings were common usage in any language, then there must be some good underlying cause behind it; that set me off in search of my Guide the Lama Mingyar Dondup.

"Honourable Lama!" I burst into his study in some excitement. He looked up at me not at all perturbed at my unceremonious entry. "Honourable Lama, why do we use colours to describe moods?" He put down the book which he was studying and motioned for me to be seated. "I suppose you are meaning those common usage terms about a blue mood, or a man green with envy?" he queried. "Yes," I answered in even more excitement, excitement that he should know precisely what I was referring to. "I really would like to know why all these colours are important. There must be something behind it!" He looked at me and laughed again, retorting, "Well, Lobsang, you have let yourself in for another nice long lecture. But I see that you have been doing some strenuous exercise and I think that you and I might have tea—I was waiting for mine anyhow—before we go on with this subject." Tea was not long in coming. This time it was tea and tsampa, the same as any other monk or lama or boy in the whole of the Lamasery would be having. We ate in silence, I thinking about colours and wondering what the implication of colours would be. Soon we had finished our rather meagre meal, and I looked at my Guide expectantly.

"You know a little about musical instruments, Lobsang," he commenced, "you know, for example, that there is a musical instrument much used in the West known as a piano. You will remember that together we looked at a picture of one. It contains a keyboard with a lot of notes on it, some black and some white, well, let us forget the black ones, let us imagine instead that we have got a keyboard perhaps two miles long—longer if you like—it contains every vibration which can be obtained on any plane of existence." He looked at me to see if I was following, because a piano was a strange device as far as I was concerned. I—as my Guide had said—had seen such a thing only in pictures. Satisfied that I could perceive the underlying idea, he continued, "If you had a keyboard containing every vibration, then the whole range of human vibrations would be in perhaps the three middle keys. You will understand—at least I hope you will!—that everything consists of vibrations. Let us take the lowest vibration known to man. The lowest vibration is that of a hard material. You touch it and it obstructs the passage of your finger, at the same time all its molecules are vibrating! You can go further up the imaginary keyboard, and you can hear a vibration known as sound. You can go higher and your eyes can receive a vibration which is known as sight."

I jerked bolt upright at that; how could sight be a vibration? If I looked at a thing—well, *how* did I see? "You see, Lobsang, because the article which is being viewed vibrates and creates a commotion which is perceived by the eye. In other words, an article which you can see generates a wave which can be received by the rods and cones in the eye which in turn translates the impulses received to a portion of the brain which converts the impulses into a picture of the original article. It is all very complicated, and we do not want to go into it too thoroughly. I am merely trying to point out to you that everything is a vibration. If we go higher up the scale we have radio waves, telepathic waves, and the waves of those people who live on other planes. But, of course, I said that we are going to limit ourselves specifically to the mythical three notes on the keyboard which could be perceived by humans as a solid thing, as a sound, or as a sight." I had to think about all this, it was a matter which really made my brain buzz. I never minded learning, however, by the kind methods of my Guide. The only time I jibbed at learning was when some tyrannical teacher was whacking away at my poor old robe with a thoroughly unpleasant stick.

"You ask about colours, Lobsang. Well, certain vibrations are impressed upon one's aura as colours. Thus, by way of example, if a person is feeling miserable—if he is feeling thoroughly unhappy—then part of his senses will emit a vibration or frequency which approximates to the colour which we call blue, so that even people who are not clairvoyant can almost perceive the blueness, and so that colour has crept into most languages throughout the world as indicating a blue mood—an unpleasant, unhappy mood." I was beginning to get the drift of the idea now, but it still puzzled me how a person could be green with envy, and I said so. "Lobsang, by deduction you should have been able to reason for yourself that when a person is suffering from the vice known as envy his vibrations change somewhat so that he gives the impression to others of being green. I do not mean that his features turn green, as you are well aware, but he does give the impression of being green. I should also make it clear to you that when a person is born under a certain planetary influence, then he is affected more strongly by those colours." "Yes!" I burst out, "I know that a person born under Aries likes red!" My Guide laughed at my eagerness and said, "Yes, that comes under the law of harmonics. Certain people respond more readily to a certain colour because the vibration of that colour is in close sympathy with their own basic vibration. That is why an Aries person (for example) prefers a red colour—because the Aries person has much red in his make-up and he finds the colour red itself pleasant to dwell upon."

I was bursting to ask a question; I knew about these greens and blues, I could even make out why a person should be in a brown study—because when a person was concentrating on a particular form of study his aura perhaps would be irridated with brown flecks. But I could not understand why a woman should be scarlet! "Honourable Lama!" I burst out, unable to contain my curiosity any longer, "why can a woman be called a scarlet woman?" My Guide looked at me as if he was going to burst and I wondered for a moment what I had said which had caused him to nearly throw a fit with suppressed amusement, then he told me, kindly and in some detail so that in future I should not be so unclear on any subject!

"I want also to tell you, Lobsang, that every person has a basic frequency of vibration, that is, every person's molecules vibrate at a certain rate and the wave length generated by a person's brain can fall into special groups. No two persons have the same wave length—not the same wave length identical in every respect, but when two people are near the same wave length, or when their wavelength follows certain octaves of the other, then they are said to be compatible and they usually get on very well together." I looked at him and wondered about some of our highly temperamental artists. "Honourable Lama, is it true that some of the artists vibrate at a higher rate than others?" I enquired. "Most certainly it is, Lobsang," said my Guide, "if a man is to have what is known as inspiration, if he is to be a good artist, then his frequency of vibrations must be many times higher than normal. Sometimes it makes him irritable—difficult to get on with. Being of a higher rate of vibration than most of us he tends to look down on us lesser mortals. However, often the work that he turns out is so good that we can put up with his slight fads and fancies!"

I imagined this great keyboard stretching for several miles, and it did seem to me a strange thing if, in a keyboard stretching several miles, the human range of experiences would be limited only to about three notes, and I said so. "The human being, Lobsang, likes to think that he is the only thing in creation that is important, you know. Actually there are many many other forms of life besides humans. On other planets there are forms of life which are utterly alien to humans, and the average human could not even begin to understand such a form of life. On our mythical keyboard the inhabitants of a planet far far removed from this particular Universe would be right away at a different end of the keyboard from that of the humans. Again, people on the astral planes of existence would be higher up the keyboard, for a ghost who can walk through a wall is of such a tenuous nature that his own rate of vibrations would be high indeed although his molecular content would be low." He looked at me and laughed at my puzzled expression, and then explained, "Well, you see, a ghost can pass through a stone wall because a stone wall consists of molecules in vibration. There are spaces between every molecule, and if you can get a creature with molecules so small that they can fit between the spaces of a stone wall, then that particular creature would be able to walk through a stone wall with no obstruction whatever. Of course, the astral creatures have a very high rate of vibration, and they are of a tenuous nature, that is, they are not solid, which in its turn means that they have few molecules. Most people imagine that the space beyond our earth—beyond the edge of the air above us—is empty. That is not so, space has molecules throughout. They are mostly hydrogen molecules which are widely dispersed, but the molecules are there and they can indeed be measured in much the same way as can the presence of a so-called ghost be measured." The Temple conches sounded, calling us once again to our Services. "We will talk about this again tomorrow, Lobsang, because I want you to be very clear on this subject," said my Guide as we parted at the entrance to the Temple.

The ending of the Temple Service was the start of a race—a race to get food. We were all rather hungry for our own food supplies were exhausted. This was the day when a new supply of freshly roasted barley was available. In Tibet all monks carry a small leather pouch of barley which has been roasted and ground and which, by the addition of buttered tea, becomes tsampa. So we raced on, and soon joined the throng waiting to have their bags filled, then we went to the Hall where tea was available so that we could have our evening meal.

The stuff was terrible. I chewed at my tsampa and wondered if my stomach was wrong. There was a horrible, oily burnt taste to it, and I really did not know how I was going to get it down. "Faugh!" muttered the boy next to me, "this stuff has been burnt to a frazzle, none of us will be able to cram it down!" "It seems to me that everything has been spoiled in this lot of food!" I said. I tried a bit more, screwing up my face in anxious concentration—wondering how I was going to cram it down. In Tibet to

216

waste such food is a great offence. I looked about me, and saw that others were looking about them! The tsampa was bad, there was no doubt about that. Everywhere bowls were being put down and that was a very rare occurrence in our community where everyone was always just on the point of hunger. I hastily swallowed the tsampa in my mouth, and something very strange about it hit me with unexpected force in the stomach. Hastily scrambling to my feet, and apprehensively holding my mouth with my hand, I bolted for the door . . . !

"Well! Young man," said a strangely accented voice as I turned back toward the door after having violently erupted the disturbing food. I turned and saw Kenji Tekeuchi, the Japanese monk who had been everywhere, seen everything, and done everything, and was now paying for it by way of periodic bouts of mental instability. He looked sympathetically at me, "Vile stuff, isn't it?" he remarked sympathetically, "I had the same difficulty as you and I came out here for the same reason. We shall have to see what happens. I am staying out for a few moments hoping that the fresh air will blow away some of the miasma which this bad food has caused." "Sir!" I said diffidently, "you have been everywhere, and will you tell me why here in Tibet we have such dreadfully monotonous fare? I am sick to death of tsampa and tea, and tea and tsampa, and tsampa and tea. Sometimes I can hardly cram the muck down."

The Japanese looked at me with great understanding and even greater sympathy. "Ah! So you ask me because I have tasted so many different kinds of food? Yes, and so I have. I have travelled extensively throughout the whole of my life. I have had food in England, Germany, Russia —almost everywhere that you can mention. In spite of my priestly vows I have lived well, or at least I thought so at the time, but now my dereliction from my vows has brought me to grief." He looked at me and then seemed to jerk to life again. "Oh! Yes! You ask why you have such monotonous fare. I will tell you. People in the West eat too much, and they have too great a variety of food, the digestive organs work on an involuntary basis, that is, they are not controlled by the voluntary part of the brain. As we teach, if the brain through the eyes has an opportunity of assessing the type of food which is going to be consumed, then the stomach can release the necessary quantity and concentration of gastric juices in order to deal with the food. If, on the other hand, everything is crammed down indiscriminately, and the consumer is busily engaged in idle talk all the time, then the juices are not prepared, digestion cannot be accomplished, and the poor wretch suffers from indigestion and later, perhaps, from gastric ulcers. You want to know why your food is plain? Well! The plainer and, within reason, the more monotonous the food one consumes the better it is for the development of the psychic parts of the body. I was a great student of the Occult, I had great powers of clairvoyance, and then I stuffed myself with all sorts of incredible concoctions and even more incredible drinks. I lost all my metaphysical powers, so that now I have come here to the Chakpori so that I may be attended, so that I may have a place where I can rest my weary body before leaving this earth. And when I have left this earth in just a few short months from now, the body breakers will do the job—will complete the task—which an indiscriminate admixture of drinks and food started." He looked at me and then gave one of those queer jumps again, and said, "Oh yes, my boy! You take my advice, you stick to plain food for all the days of your life and you will never lose your powers. Go against my advice and cram everything you can down your hungry gullet, and you will lose everything, and your gain? Well, my boy, you will gain indigestion; you will gain gastric ulcers together with a bad temper. Oh ho! I am going off, I can feel another attack coming." The Japanese monk, Kenji Tekeuchi rose shakily to his feet and tottered off in the direction of the Lamas' Quarters. I looked after him and shook my head sadly. I should very much have liked to have been able to talk to him much longer. What sort of foods were they? Did they taste good? Then I pulled myself up with a jerk; why tantalise myself when all I had before me was rancid buttered tea and tsampa which had been really burned so much that it was a charred mass, and in some way some strange oily compound had got into it. I shook my head and walked again into the Hall.

Later in the evening I was talking to my Guide, the Lama Mingyar Dondup. "Honourable Lama, why do people buy horoscopes from the pedlars down on The Way?" My Guide smiled sadly as he replied, "Of course, as you know, there cannot be any worthwhile horoscope unless it is individually prepared for the person to whom it is alleged to refer. No horoscope can be prepared on a mass production basis. The horoscopes sold by the pedlars on The Road below are merely so that they can get money from the credulous." He looked at me and said, "Of course, Lobsang, the pilgrims who have these horoscopes go back home and show they have a momento from the Potala! They are satisfied and so is the pedlar so why bother about them? Everyone is satisfied." "Do you think people should have horoscopes prepared for them?" I asked. "Not really, Lobsang, not really. Only in certain cases such as your own case. Too often horoscopes are merely used to save a person the effort of adopting a course of action upon his own responsibility. I am very much against the use of astrology or horoscopes unless there is a definite, specific reason for it. As you know, the average person is like a pilgrim threading his way through the City of Lhasa. He cannot see the road ahead for the trees and the houses and the bends and curves in the road. He has to be prepared for whatever is coming. We here can look down upon the road and see any obstruction for we are at a higher elevation. The pilgrim, then, is like a person with no horoscope. We being higher in the air than the pilgrim are like people with the horoscope, for we can see the road ahead, we can see obstacles and difficulties, and thus should be in a position to overcome difficulties before they really occur."

"There is another thing which is troubling me greatly, Honourable Lama. Can you tell me how it is that we know things in this life that we knew in the past?" I looked at him most anxiously for I was always rather afraid of asking such questions as really I had no right to be delving so deeply into matters, but he took no offence, instead he replied, "Before we came to this earth, Lobsang, we mapped out what we intended to do. The knowledge was stored in our subconscious and if we could get in touch with our subconscious—as some of us can!—then we should know everything that we had planned. Of course, if we should know everything that we had planned there would be no merit in striving to better ourselves because we would know that we were working along a predetermined plan. For some reasons sometimes a person will go to sleep or will get out of the body while conscious, and will get in touch with his Overself. Sometimes the Overself will be able to bring up knowledge from the subconscious and transfer it back to the body on earth, so that when the astral body returns to the flesh body there is knowledge in the mind of certain things that happened in a past life. It may be as a special warning not to commit a mistake which may have been committed for life after life. Sometimes a person has a great desire to commit suicide—as just for example—and if a person has been penalised life after life for doing that, then frequently they will have a memory of something about self-destruction in the hope that such a memory will cause the body to refrain from self-destruction."

I pondered upon all this and then I walked to the window and looked out. Just below there was the fresh green of the swampy area and the beautiful green of the leaves of the willow trees. My Guide broke into my reverie. "You like looking out of this window, Lobsang, does it occur to you that you look out so frequently because you find the green so soothing to your eyes?" As I thought about it I realised that I did instinctively see green after I had been working at my books. "Green, Lobsang, is the most restful colour for the eyes. It gives ease to tired eyes. When you go to the Western world you will find that in some of their theatres there is a place called the green room where actors and actresses go to rest their eyes after having been subjected to smoke-filled stages and bright glaring footlights and floodlights." I opened my eyes in amazement at this, and I decided that I would pursue this matter of colours whenever the opportunity presented itself. My Guide said, "I have to leave you now, Lobsang, but tomorrow come to me again because I am going to teach you some other things." He rose to his feet, patted me on the shoulder, and went out. For some time I stood looking out of the window looking out at the green of the swamp grass and the trees which were so restful to the eyes.

CHAPTER TWELVE

I stood a little way down the path, looking down the mountainside. My heart was sick within me and my eyes were hot with the tears I dare not shed. The old man was being carried down the mountain. The Japanese monk, Kenji Tekeuchi, had "returned to his Ancestors." Now the Disposers of the Dead were carrying his poor shrivelled old body away from us. Was his Spirit even now wandering on a path lined with cherry blossoms? Or was he seeing the mistakes of his lifetime and planning his return? I looked down again before the men rounded a curve in the path. Looked down at the pathetic bundle that once had been a man. A shadow came over the sun, and for a time I imagined that I saw a face in the clouds.

Was it true, I wondered, that there were Guardians of the World? Great Spirit Guardians who saw to it that Man had suffering on Earth in order to live. Why, they must be like schoolteachers, I thought! Perhaps Kenji Tekeuchi would meet them. Perhaps he would be told that he had learned well. I hoped so, for he had been a frail old man who had seen much and suffered much. Or would he have to come down to the flesh again—reincarnate—so that he could learn more? When would he come? In some six hundred years, or now?

I thought of it; I thought of the service I had just left. The Service for Guiding the Dead. The flickering butter-lamps, flickering like the flames of a feeble life. I thought of the clouds of sweet-smelling incense which seemed to form into living creatures. For a moment I had thought Kenji Tekeuchi had come among us again as a living being instead of propped up before us as a wizened corpse. Now perhaps he would be looking at the Akashic Record, that indelible Record of all that has ever happened. Maybe he would be able to see where he had gone wrong and remember for when he came again.

The old man had taught me a lot. In his strange way he had been fond of me, talking to me as an equal. Now he was no more on the Earth. Idly I kicked a stone and scuffed my worn sandals in the ground. Had he a mother? Somehow I could not imagine him as young, as having a family. He must have been lonely, living among us strangers, so far from his own land. So far from the warm breezes and his own Sacred Mountain. Often he had told me about Japan, and then his voice had grown hoarse and his eyes strange.

One day he had shocked me by saying that people probed into occult matters when they would be better off by waiting until they were ready, instead of trying to importune a Master. "The Master *always* comes when the Student is ready, boy!" he said to me, "and when you have a Master—do everything he says, for only then are you ready." The day was becoming duller. Clouds were forming overhead and the wind was beginning to whip up small stones again.

Below me, in the Plain, a small group of men appeared from the base of the mountain. Gently they placed their pathetic bundle on the back of a pony, mounted their own, and slowly rode off. I stared out across the Plain, until at last the small cortege vanished from my sight. Slowly I turned away and trudged up the mountain.